**OPPOSING
VIEWPOINTS®
SERIES**

Congressional Ethics

Other Books of Related Interest:

Opposing Viewpoints Series

The Federal Budget

Judicial Activism

Presidential Powers

The US Deficit

At Issue Series

Campaign Finance

The Federal Budget Deficit

How Does Religion Influence Politics?

Voter Fraud

Current Controversies Series

Capitalism

Federal Elections

Politics and the Media

The Tea Party Movement

US Government Corruption

"Congress shall make no law ... abridging the freedom of speech, or of the press."

First Amendment to the US Constitution

The basic foundation of our democracy is the First Amendment guarantee of freedom of expression. The Opposing Viewpoints series is dedicated to the concept of this basic freedom and the idea that it is more important to practice it than to enshrine it.

**OPPOSING
VIEWPOINTS®
SERIES**

Congressional Ethics

Joe Tardiff and Lynn M. Zott, Book Editors

GREENHAVEN PRESS
A part of Gale, Cengage Learning

GALE
CENGAGE Learning·

Detroit • New York • San Francisco • New Haven, Conn • Waterville, Maine • London

Elizabeth Des Chenes, *Director, Publishing Solutions*

For more information, contact:
Greenhaven Press
27500 Drake Rd.
Farmington Hills, MI 48331-3535
Or you can visit our Internet site at gale.cengage.com

LIBRARY OF CONGRESS CATALOGING-IN-PUBLICATION DATA

Congressional ethics / Joe Tardiff and Lynn M. Zott, book editors.
    p. cm. -- (Opposing viewpoints)
Summary: "Opposing Viewpoints: Congressional Ethics: Opposing Viewpoints is the leading source for libraries and classrooms in need of current-issue materials. The viewpoints are selected from a wide range of highly respected sources and publications" -- Provided by publisher.
    Includes bibliographical references and index.
    ISBN 978-0-7377-6046-0 -- ISBN 978-0-7377-6047-7 (pbk.)
    1. United States. Congress--Ethics--Juvenile literature. 2. Political ethics--United States--Juvenile literature. I. Tardiff, Joseph C., 1966- II. Zott, Lynn M. (Lynn Marie), 1969-
    JK1121.C664 2012
    172'.2--dc23

                                                        2012031899

Printed in the United States of America
1 2 3 4 5   17 16 15 14 13

Contents

Chapter 4: What Are Some Consequences of Ethics Violations?

Why Consider Opposing Viewpoints?

> *"The only way in which a human being can make some approach to knowing the whole of a subject is by hearing what can be said about it by persons of every variety of opinion and studying all modes in which it can be looked at by every character of mind. No wise man ever acquired his wisdom in any mode but this."*
>
> John Stuart Mill

In our media-intensive culture it is not difficult to find differing opinions. Thousands of newspapers and magazines and dozens of radio and television talk shows resound with differing points of view. The difficulty lies in deciding which opinion to agree with and which "experts" seem the most credible. The more inundated we become with differing opinions and claims, the more essential it is to hone critical reading and thinking skills to evaluate these ideas. Opposing Viewpoints books address this problem directly by presenting stimulating debates that can be used to enhance and teach these skills. The varied opinions contained in each book examine many different aspects of a single issue. While examining these conveniently edited opposing views, readers can develop critical thinking skills such as the ability to compare and contrast authors' credibility, facts, argumentation styles, use of persuasive techniques, and other stylistic tools. In short, the Opposing Viewpoints Series is an ideal way to attain the higher-level thinking and reading skills so essential in a culture of diverse and contradictory opinions.

In addition to providing a tool for critical thinking, Opposing Viewpoints books challenge readers to question their own strongly held opinions and assumptions. Most people form their opinions on the basis of upbringing, peer pressure, and personal, cultural, or professional bias. By reading carefully balanced opposing views, readers must directly confront new ideas as well as the opinions of those with whom they disagree. This is not to argue simplistically that everyone who reads opposing views will—or should—change his or her opinion. Instead, the series enhances readers' understanding of their own views by encouraging confrontation with opposing ideas. Careful examination of others' views can lead to the readers' understanding of the logical inconsistencies in their own opinions, perspective on why they hold an opinion, and the consideration of the possibility that their opinion requires further evaluation.

Evaluating Other Opinions

To ensure that this type of examination occurs, Opposing Viewpoints books present all types of opinions. Prominent spokespeople on different sides of each issue as well as well-known professionals from many disciplines challenge the reader. An additional goal of the series is to provide a forum for other, less known, or even unpopular viewpoints. The opinion of an ordinary person who has had to make the decision to cut off life support from a terminally ill relative, for example, may be just as valuable and provide just as much insight as a medical ethicist's professional opinion. The editors have two additional purposes in including these less known views. One, the editors encourage readers to respect others' opinions—even when not enhanced by professional credibility. It is only by reading or listening to and objectively evaluating others' ideas that one can determine whether they are worthy of consideration. Two, the inclusion of such viewpoints encourages the important critical thinking skill of objectively evaluating an author's credentials and bias. This evaluation will illuminate an author's reasons for taking a particular stance on an issue and will aid in readers' evaluation of the author's ideas.

It is our hope that these books will give readers a deeper understanding of the issues debated and an appreciation of the complexity of even seemingly simple issues when good and honest people disagree. This awareness is particularly important in a democratic society such as ours in which people enter into public debate to determine the common good. Those with whom one disagrees should not be regarded as enemies but rather as people whose views deserve careful examination and may shed light on one's own.

Thomas Jefferson once said that "difference of opinion leads to inquiry, and inquiry to truth." Jefferson, a broadly educated man, argued that "if a nation expects to be ignorant and free . . . it expects what never was and never will be." As individuals and as a nation, it is imperative that we consider the opinions of others and examine them with skill and discernment. The Opposing Viewpoints series is intended to help readers achieve this goal.

David L. Bender and Bruno Leone,
Founders

Introduction

> *"The aim of every political institution is, or ought to be, first to obtain for rulers men who possess the most wisdom to discern, and most virtue to pursue, the common good of society; and in the next place, to take the most effectual precautions for keeping them virtuous whilst they continue to hold their public trust."*
>
> —James Madison,
> "Federalist No. 57," 1788

When American voters elect a candidate to represent them in the United States Congress, they expect that elected official to meet certain fundamental standards of ethical integrity. Indeed, most elected officials are able to navigate with success the murky waters of federal campaign financing, the influence of special interest groups, and potential abuses of office by adhering to the rules and regulations outlined in the Code of Official Conduct for both the House of Representatives and the Senate. However, it seems more often than not that news surfaces about the public exposure of a lawmaker who becomes embroiled in an illegal campaign financing scheme, who is at the center of an investigation into his or her abuse of public office, or who is caught up in a media firestorm surrounding a sordid sex scandal.

Both the House of Representatives and the Senate have permanent committees that are responsible for investigating and, if necessary, recommending disciplinary action for members of Congress who engage in ethical misconduct. However, the results achieved by these committees are often less than satisfactory to the American public because there is a lack of transparency in the investigation proceedings; investigations become mired in governmental bureaucracy; and ultimately, most violators only receive a mild rebuke for their misconduct. Two recent cases—ethics investigations into the questionable activities of Representatives Vern Buchanan (a Republican from Florida) and Shelley Berkley (a Democrat from Nevada)—illustrate the problems and pitfalls surrounding the investigation and punishment of elected officials who commit ethics violations in Congress today.

Questions of ethical, and even illegal, wrongdoing have followed Vern Buchanan since his 2006 campaign for the House of Representatives. Prior to his election to Congress, Buchanan made millions of dollars as a real estate developer and as the owner of several auto dealerships in the Sarasota area. Issues surrounding his ethical integrity first arose when he was accused of directing employees and business associates to make substantial cash donations to his 2006 election campaign; allegedly, these contributors were then reimbursed for their donation out of corporate funds from Buchanan's auto dealerships. Buchanan was also accused of witness tampering, coercion, and attempted bribery when he allegedly sought to persuade a former business partner not to testify against him in a Federal Election Commission (FEC) investigation into the donation reimbursement scheme. More recently, the Office of Congressional Ethics (OCE) announced that it was investigating Buchanan for failing to include in financial disclosure documents required by the House income earned from seventeen positions at six different organizations between 2007 and 2010.

Despite Buchanan's numerous alleged ethics violations, he has yet to be disciplined for any infraction. The FEC investigation into the illegal campaign financing scheme concluded with no charges being filed against Buchanan. While the OCE continues to investigate the circumstances surrounding Buchanan's failure to disclose all of his financial dealings, most observers believe that this probe, too, will end once

Buchanan files an amended disclosure statement with the House. Dismayed by the lack of action taken on the reimbursement scheme in particular, Citizens for Responsibility and Ethics in Washington (CREW), a nonprofit government watchdog agency, asked the Federal Bureau of Investigation (FBI) to investigate the allegations of wrongdoing. This request prompted the Department of Justice to open a probe into Buchanan's connection with the money laundering scheme. Despite the ongoing investigation, Buchanan continued to campaign for reelection in 2012.

In 2011 Rep. Shelley Berkley also faced charges of ethical misconduct for alleged abuses of power and conflict of interest through her aggressive advocacy of kidney care that ultimately benefits the financial interests of her husband, prominent nephrologist Dr. Lawrence Lehrner. The allegations of abuse of office chiefly centered on Berkley's intervention in the Centers for Medicare & Medicaid Services' (CMS) decision to shut down the kidney transplant program at the University Medical Center of Southern Nevada (UMC) in 2008. CMS's decision to cut funding largely was based on the unusually high incidence rate of kidney rejections and patient deaths that occurred in the transplant program. The proposed termination of funding would have had a detrimental impact on the profit margins of Kidney Specialists of Southern Nevada (KSSN)—run by Lehrner—which provided training and medical support for the transplant program. Berkley's prominent role in reaching a compromise with CMS to keep the kidney transplant program open not only preserved KSSN's existing business interests, but it also led to CMS awarding KSSN a new sole-bidder contract worth $738,000 per year to add resources to the program. In a report published in the *Las Vegas Review-Journal* on September 14, 2011, Berkley commented on the apparent conflict of interest: "I recognized no matter what I chose to do, somebody would have thought it was not the right thing. I recognize that it may not look great, but I recognized that the kidney transplant center was worth fighting for."

In another case, Berkley opposed efforts by CMS to cut government reimbursement rates to dialysis providers by 3.1 percent in 2011. She persuaded seventy-three other House members to sign a letter urging the President Barack Obama administration to change its position on the rate cut—a request to which the administration promptly acceded. To reward her ongoing support, numerous organizations in the kidney care industry—including DaVita, a joint partnership in which her husband owns a substantial share—have donated more than $140,000 to her reelection campaigns over the years.

As with a traditional legal case, it is sometimes difficult to prove with reasonable certainty that accused members of Congress are guilty of ethics violations. In Buchanan's case, the evidence implicating him in ethical misconduct is compromised by the perceived unreliability of the witnesses who have testified against him: disgruntled ex-employees, jilted business partners, and political enemies. In Berkley's case, allegations of abuse of office are counterbalanced by the fact that she was acting on behalf of her constituents when she lobbied to prevent the federal government from shutting down the only kidney transplant center in Nevada. What is clear is that the internal investigation process into ethical misconduct is often hindered by partisan gamesmanship, plodding bureaucracy, and a general lack of transparency. Oftentimes, it is up to external watchdog groups and news organizations to step in and pressure a reluctant Congress to investigate the unethical behavior of its members with due diligence.

OVP: Congressional Ethics explores issues raised in this introduction regarding the definition of ethical misconduct, the effectiveness of Congress's ability to police itself, and the consequences—or lack thereof—for congressional members who engage in unethical behavior. Viewpoints offering differing perspective on congressional ethics are organized into the following chapters: Is the Congressional Ethical Oversight System Necessary and Effective?, What Impact Do Congressional Ethics Have on Social and Political Issues?, How Does Lobbying and Ethics Reform Legislation Affect Ethics?, and What Are Some Consequences of Ethics Violations? Given the sheer complexity of legislative proposals in the present day, the corruptive influence of special interest groups that lobby lawmakers incessantly, and the trillions of federal tax dollars being appropriated and spent by members of Congress each year, an in-depth understanding of the issues surrounding congressional ethics can provide valuable insight into the function of the American government in the twenty-first century.

CHAPTER 1

Is the Congressional Ethical Oversight System Necessary and Effective?

Chapter Preface

In the US Congress, the process that involves the oversight, investigation, and punishment of ethics violations committed by the body's members often involves reluctant self-policing, opportunistic partisan maneuvering, and plodding bureaucracy. If found guilty of any ethical impropriety that does not break the law, a member of the House of Representatives or the Senate typically receives merely a token reprimand from his or her colleagues in either institution. Discipline may include public censure on the floor of the institution; a warning; and in some circumstances, suspension from the legislature. In extremely rare cases, a member of Congress who is found guilty of serious ethics violations can be removed from office. However, only a few expulsions from either the House or the Senate have ever occurred—besides the removal of a dozen or so Confederate supporters during the Civil War.

Both the House and Senate have committees that are responsible for investigating the alleged ethics infractions of their members. However, the proceedings of these committees are shrouded in secrecy, so outside parties generally are not provided with information on the specific ethics charges leveled at a member, the details surrounding the investigation, or the evidence that leads to either punishment or exoneration. Sometimes, partisan gamesmanship can corrupt what should be an impartial examination of ethics violations, as was the case in 2011 when staff members of the Office of Congressional Ethics (OCE) were accused of improperly releasing confidential information on an investigation into the ethical conduct of Democratic representative Maxine Waters to Republican members of the House ethics committee. As a result, the Republican members of the committee disqualified themselves from the case for conflict of interest and an outside special investigator had to be appointed to continue the investigation.

Another factor that interferes with the successful prosecution of ethics violators in Congress is the protracted pace of the investigations. Indeed, many members who have been charged with ethics infractions have exploited the system to their advantage by denying any wrongdoing, refusing to cooperate with investigators, and withholding potentially incriminating documentation as long as possible in order to delay the investigation. In many cases, congressional members under investigation will choose to resign before any formal disciplinary measures can be enacted. Still others are able to serve out the remainder of their term of office while awaiting the results of a long, deliberative inquiry. In either case, unless a law has been broken that would require the investigative panel to forward the matter to law enforcement, ethics committees in both the House and Senate promptly suspend the investigation if the accused member leaves office.

Oftentimes the responsibility for publicizing and investigating an ethics scandal falls to external entities such as the news media or government watchdog organizations. While the news media play a crucial role in making the public aware of alleged ethical misconduct, these organizations are frequently driven by ratings rather than any principled desire to expose an injustice. As a result, when a news story surrounding a scandal begins to cool off, media outlets typically devote less print or airtime to the topic and instead focus on the next big story. Politicians are acutely aware of the short life span of a news story, and they are masters at employing stalling tactics to keep the media at bay until an incriminating story recedes from the public consciousness. However, in exceptional cases, such as the Anthony Weiner "sexting" scandal in 2011, the media scrutiny becomes so intense and the public embarrassment so overwhelming, that the offender has no choice but to resign from office in disgrace.

Like the media, government watchdog groups perform an important oversight function when it comes to holding public officials accountable for their questionable ethical conduct. Groups such as the Campaign Legal Center, Citizens for Responsibility and Ethics in Washington (CREW), and the Institute for Global Ethics all shine a spotlight on various forms of corruption and dishonesty in Washington, DC. These groups advocate the pursuit of a culture of positive ethical behavior in Congress, demand investigations into alleged ethics violations, and lobby for increased transparency in the operation of the federal government. Most importantly, these organizations encourage all Americans to educate themselves about the ethical values espoused by their representatives. If enough voters determine that their representative lacks integrity, then they can exercise their right to circumvent the often ineffective ethical oversight process in Congress and vote the public official out of office.

Congress's process for ethics oversight is the subject of the following chapter, which focuses on such issues as whether the ethics committees of the House and Senate are useful and needed, how much political influence they wield, and whether or not the process involved is racially biased.

"The Senate recognized that serious allegations had been made against a former employee and that it had no specific rules or regulations governing the duties and scope of activities of members, officers, and employees."

The US Senate Select Committee on Ethics Is Effective and Necessary

Select Committee on Ethics, United States Senate

In 1977 the US Senate authorized the Select Committee on Ethics to develop and implement clear rules governing the ethical conduct of the legislative body's members. The committee also possesses the power to investigate and recommend punitive action against senators who engage in unethical behavior. In the following viewpoint, the committee provides an overview of its evolution and authority, tracing its inception to a mid-twentieth-century ethics scandal involving Senate employee Robert G. "Bobby" Baker and documenting how it has evolved into an indispensable and effective monitor of ethical behavior in the Senate.

"Senate Ethics Manual, 10th Congress, 1st Session," pp. 3–12, 17–18, Select Committee on Ethics, United States Senate, 2003.

23

As you read, consider the following questions:

1. According to the viewpoint, what important document authorizes the US Congress to punish the unethical behavior of its members?

2. The questionable behavior of what employee of the Senate does the viewpoint state precipitated the drive to establish a code of ethics in 1964?

3. According to the viewpoint, have the rules governing ethical behavior in the Senate been revised or amended since the formation of the Select Committee on Ethics in 1977?

The U.S. Constitution, in Article I, Section 5, grants broad authority to Congress to discipline its members. However, the modern age of congressional ethics committees and formal rules governing the conduct of members, officers, and employees did not exist until the 1960s, with prior disciplinary actions by Congress against members taking place on an *ad hoc* basis. In 1964, in the wake of the Bobby Baker scandal [referring to Robert G. "Bobby" Baker, a Senate employee who was investigated for alleged corruption and influence peddling], the Senate adopted S. Res. 338, 88th Congress, which created the Senate Select Committee on Standards and Conduct as a six-member, bipartisan committee with advisory functions and investigative authority to "receive complaints and investigate allegations of improper conduct which may reflect upon the Senate, violations of law, and violations of rules and regulations of the Senate." In 1968, the Senate adopted its first official code of conduct, with substantial revision and amendment of the code occurring in 1977. The committee's name was changed in 1977 to the Select Committee on Ethics [also known as the Senate Ethics Committee]. . . .

The Select Committee on Standards and Conduct was established by the Senate on July 24, 1964. In February 1977, following Senate-wide committee reorganization, its name was changed to the Select Committee on Ethics. The bipartisan committee, which has six members, is authorized to oversee the Senate's self-discipline authority provided by the Constitution. Article I, Section 5 states in part that:

Each House may determine the rules of its proceedings, punish its members for disorderly behavior, and, with the concurrence of two-thirds, expel a member.

Ethics Committee Given Broad Powers

The committee is authorized to:

1. receive complaints and investigate allegations of improper conduct which may reflect upon the Senate, violations of law, violations of the Senate Code of Official Conduct, and violations of rules and regulations of the Senate, relating to the conduct of individuals in the performance of their duties as members of the Senate, or as officers or employees of the Senate, and to make appropriate findings of fact and conclusions with respect thereto;

2. recommend, when appropriate, disciplinary action against members and staff;

3. recommend rules or regulations necessary to insure appropriate Senate standards of conduct;

4. report violations of any law to the proper federal and state authorities;

5. regulate the use of the franking [mailing items for free] privilege in the Senate;

6. investigate unauthorized disclosures of intelligence information;

7. implement the Senate public financial disclosure requirements of the Ethics in Government Act;

8. regulate the receipt and disposition of gifts from foreign governments received by members, officers, and employees of the Senate;

9. render advisory opinions on the application of Senate rules and laws to members, officers, and employees; and

10. for complaints filed under the Government Employee Rights Act of 1991 respecting conduct occurring prior to January 23, 1996, review, upon request, any decision of the Office of Senate Fair Employment Practices.

The committee may investigate allegations brought by members, officers, or employees of the Senate, or by any other individual or group, or the committee may initiate an inquiry on its own. There are no formal procedural requirements for filing a complaint with the committee. Unless the committee issues a public statement relating to a particular inquiry, complaints and allegations are treated confidentially, and the committee neither confirms nor denies that a particular matter may be before the committee. Upon completion of its investigative process, the committee may recommend to the Senate or party conference an appropriate sanction for a violation or improper conduct, including, for senators, censure, expulsion, or party discipline and, for staff members, termination of employment. . . .

The Bobby Baker Investigation

Momentum for reform grew after Robert G. (Bobby) Baker, secretary to the Democratic majority, resigned from his job in October 1963 following allegations that he had misused his official position for personal financial gain. For the next year and a half, the Senate Rules and Administration Committee held hearings to investigate the business interests and activities of Senate officials and employees (focused on Bobby Baker) in order to ascertain what, if any, conflicts of interest or other improprieties existed and whether any additional laws or regulations were needed. The Senate recognized that serious allegations had been made against a former employee and that it had no specific rules or regulations governing the duties and scope of activities of members, officers, and employees.

In its first report, the Rules Committee characterized many of Baker's outside activities as being in conflict with his official duties and made several recommendations, including adoption of public financial disclosure rules and other guidelines for senatorial employees.

Subsequently, as part of its conclusion of the Baker case, the Rules Committee held additional hearings on proposals advocating a code of ethics in conjunction with a pending pay raise, the creation of a joint congressional ethics committee to write an ethics code, and the adoption of various rules requiring public disclosure of personal finances by senators and staff and the disclosure of ex parte communications. Additions to the Senate rules—calling for public financial disclosure reports and more controls on staff involvement in Senate campaign funds—were then introduced to implement the committee's Baker investigation recommendations.

The Rules Committee concluded that remedial action was necessary to make those who serve the public "recognize that their office is a public trust and should not be compromised by private interests." To this end, the committee recommended the adoption of financial disclosure rules, the development of guidelines for committees and staff, and the executive branch's consideration of public record keeping of congressional intervention on matters pending before agencies.

The First Ethics Committee Is Formed

In July 1964, the Rules Committee reported Senate Resolution 338, 88th Congress, which would have amended Senate Rule XXV to give the Rules Committee jurisdiction "to investigate every alleged violation of the rules of the Senate, and to make appropriate findings of fact and conclusions" and to "recommend appropriate disciplinary action as may be indicated by the particular circumstances of individual instances."

The Senate took up S. Res. 338 first. Senator John Sherman Cooper, one of the members of the Rules Committee who had been dissatisfied with the Baker investigation, introduced a substitute resolution, proposing the establishment of a permanent Select Committee on Standards and Conduct to "investigate allegations of improper conduct which may reflect upon the Senate, violations of law, and violations of rules and regulations of the Senate, relating to the conduct of individuals in the performance of their duties as members of the Senate, or as officers or employees of the Senate," and to make "recommendation[s] to the Senate [of] appropriate disciplinary action.". . .

A section of the Cooper substitute authorizing the committee to investigate "allegations of improper conduct" received particular attention. Senator Clifford Case stated his understanding that under this section "the committee would be free to investigate anything which, in its judgment, seemed worthy, deserving, and requiring investigation from any source." After Senator Cooper confirmed this interpretation, Senator Case expressed his support for the substitute, noting that "unlike the resolution in its original form, . . . the proposal would not be limited to alleged violations of Senate rules, but it would take into account all improper conduct of any kind whatsoever." The Senate agreed to the Cooper substitute and adopted S. Res. 338 by a vote of 61 to 19 on July 24, 1964. With the creation of this committee, an internal disciplinary body was established in Congress for the first time on a continuing basis.

The six members of the new committee were not appointed until a year later, July 9, 1965, because of the Senate leadership's desire to wait until the Rules Committee had completed the Baker investigation. It was not until October 1965 that the committee elected a chairman and a vice chairman, appointed the first staff, and began developing standards of conduct for the Senate. The committee's initial efforts in this regard were interrupted by its investigation of Senator Thomas Dodd. Following that investigation, the committee returned to the development of ethics rules, and on March 15, 1968, reported favorably Senate Resolution 266, 90th Congress, 114 Cong. Rec. 6670 (1968), which proposed a declaration of Senate policy and four specific rules concerning ethical conduct.

The Committee Declares That Public Office Is a Public Trust

In recommending the first written internal rules of ethics for the Senate, the committee made clear that it did not intend the specific rules that it was proposing to be the Senate's exclusive source of behavioral standards. The proposed specific rules, which were set out in section two of S. Res. 266, were preceded by a declaration of Senate policy in section one of the resolution:

Resolved, It is declared to be the policy of the Senate that—

(a) The ideal concept of public office, expressed by the words, "A public office is a public trust," signifies that the officer has been entrusted with public power by the people; that the officer holds this power in trust to be used only for their benefit and never for the benefit of himself or of a few; and that the officer must never conduct his own affairs so as to infringe on the public interest. All official conduct of members of the Senate should be guided by this paramount concept of public office.

(b) These rules, as written expression of certain standards of conduct, complement the body of unwritten but generally accepted standards that continue to apply to the Senate.

The 1968 code of conduct covered four areas: outside employment of officers and employees; the raising and permissible use of campaign funds; the political fund-raising activities of Senate staff; and annual financial disclosure by members, officers, and designated employees of the Senate and senatorial candidates. With the exceptions of gifts in excess of $50 and honoraria in excess of $300, the information in the disclosure reports was to be kept confidential and not available to the public (since changed to require that statements be publicly available).

A select committee created to study the Senate committee system recommended in 1976 that the functions of the Select Committee on Standards and Conduct should be placed in the Senate Rules Committee. However, the Rules Committee rejected the idea and instead recommended a newly constituted ethics committee to indicate to the public the seriousness with which the Senate viewed congressional conduct. Thus, the permanent Select Committee on Ethics was created in 1977 to replace the Select Committee on Standards and Conduct.

The Ethics Code Is Revised and Amended

On April 1, 1977, the Senate code of conduct was revised and amended, and the procedures and duties of the ethics committee were further expanded and developed.

Title I of S. Res. 110, 95th Congress, the Official Conduct Amendments of 1977, included amendments to the Senate code of conduct first adopted in 1968. Included were the first public financial disclosure requirements for members, officers, and employees of the Senate, as well as the first limits on gifts, outside earnings, the franking privilege, the use of the Senate radio and television studios, unofficial office accounts, lameduck foreign travel, and discrimination in staff employment.

Title II amended S. Res. 338, the 1964 resolution that created the first Senate ethics committee and constituted the basic charter of the newly created Select Committee on Ethics. It provided the committee with the authority to issue regula-

The White House Ethics Website Promotes Government Transparency

President [Barack] Obama has consistently made clear that he will strive to lead the most open, transparent, and accountable government in history. For over three years, the administration has done much to make information about how government works more accessible to the public, and to solicit citizens' participation in government decision making. . . .

President Obama promised he would "create a centralized Internet database of lobbying reports, ethics records, and campaign finance filings in a searchable, sortable, and downloadable format." Today [in March 2012], with the launch of www.ethics.gov, he's delivering on that promise. In a single, user-friendly format, anyone can access and search the records of seven different databases:

- White House Visitor Records
- Office of Government Ethics Travel Reports
- Lobbying Disclosure Act Data
- Department of Justice Foreign Agents Registration Act Data
- Federal Election Commission Individual Contribution Reports
- Federal Election Commission Candidate Reports
- Federal Election Commission Committee Reports

Never before has this measure of government-verified data been available and so easily searchable in a centralized location.

"We Can't Wait: White House Launches Ethics.gov to Promote Government Accountability and Transparency," Office of the Press Secretary, March 8, 2012. www.whitehouse.gov.

tions to implement the revised code of conduct and to issue interpretative rulings to clarify its meaning and applicability. It also: 1) preserved for the ethics committee the discretion to initiate investigations; 2) set forth the procedures for the receipt and processing of sworn complaints alleging violations of any rule, law, or regulation within the committee's jurisdiction; 3) spelled out the requirement that an affirmative vote of four members of the committee is necessary for any resolution, report, recommendation, advisory opinion or investigation; 4) required the committee to adopt written rules for investigations; 5) provided for the disqualification of committee members in investigations; 6) stipulated that outside counsel must be hired for investigations unless the committee specifically decides not to use such counsel; 7) clarified that no investigation could be made of any alleged violation which was not considered a violation at the time it was alleged to have occurred; and 8) enumerated specific sanctions that the committee could recommend in calling upon the Senate to take disciplinary action.

The first years of the newly created Select Committee on Ethics were spent interpreting for the Senate the provisions of these new rules. Consequently, on February 1, 1980, the Senate adopted S. Res. 109 which directed the Select Committee on Ethics to undertake within a year a comprehensive review of the Senate Code of Official Conduct and the provisions for its enforcement, implementation, and investigation of improper conduct in the Senate.

Consultation Yields More Revision

During the course of its review, the committee held hearings in November 1980 during which academicians, federal and state ethics officials, and members of Congress testified. It sent questionnaires to senators and consulted the Hastings Center Institute of Society, Ethics, and the Life Sciences, which issued two reports.

Subsequently, the Ethics Reform Act of 1989 and the FY [fiscal year] 1992 Legislative Branch Appropriations Act significantly amended the Senate code of conduct by changing the restrictions on the acceptance of gifts and travel by members, officers, and employees of the Senate; banning honoraria; and limiting the earnings of other income by senators and designated employees.

The Senate ethics process was again the subject of careful scrutiny in 1993, when, pursuant to Senate Resolution 111 (103d Congress) creating the Senate Ethics Study Commission, hearings were held in May and June 1993 concerned solely with possible improvements in the process. In March 1994, the commission issued its report, "Recommending Revisions to the Procedures of the Senate Select Committee on Ethics." The commission's principal recommendations were adopted by the Senate on November 5, 1999, with the passage of Senate Resolution 222. . . .

Also, in July 1995, the Senate passed a new gifts rule, S. Res. 158, effective January 1, 1996, which replaced Rule 35 of the Senate code of conduct, and which further changed the restrictions on the acceptance of gifts and travel by members, officers, and employees of the Senate. . . .

The Educational and Advisory Role of the Committee

From time to time, the committee has . . . issued advice in the form of "Dear Colleague" advisory letters covering a particular subject. Additionally, over the years, the committee has issued thousands of private letter rulings to members, officers, and employees, providing advice on the application of a law or rule to a specific set of facts. . . .

The committee considers its advisory function to be among its most important. Contact with the committee about the application of laws and rules to proposed conduct is welcomed and encouraged. The committee's advisory function is conducted in a confidential manner, although advice of general applicability may be publicly disseminated in a manner which protects confidentiality. The committee's aim is to preempt possible violations by being freely accessible to provide prospective advice. . . . It is far easier to avoid a problem in advance than to correct a problem after the fact. On a number of occasions, the committee has had to advise members, officers, and employees that past conduct was not acceptable and should not be repeated, in situations where the difficulties could have been easily avoided by getting advice in advance from the committee. Routine or frequent contact with the committee for advice is encouraged.

Of course, the committee will also continue to provide advice through interpretative rulings, Dear Colleague letters, and private letter rulings on request from Senate members, officers, and employees. The committee also offers periodic briefings on the code of conduct through the secretary of the Senate's office. At least quarterly, seminars on the Code of Official Conduct are available to interested staffers, and seminars on the use of the franking privilege are separately offered. Likewise, seminars tailored for the use of office managers, committee staff, and paid interns are offered. Additionally, the committee is available at the convenience of any Senate office to provide "in-office" briefings for members or staff. Again, and perhaps most importantly, the committee is always available to Senate members, officers, and employees through its staff to provide telephonic advice and private letter rulings. Such telephone advice and private letter rulings are the mainstay of the committee's advisory function, and members, officers, and employees are encouraged to seek such advice or rulings in any situation.

There Are Many Sources of Applicable Standards of Conduct

The standards which govern a Senate member, officer, or employee's conduct, and which provide the framework for institutional discipline, are drawn from a number of sources including federal statutes and Senate rules.

Both the official and personal conduct of Senate members, officers, and employees are now the subject of a substantial body of ethics-related rules and laws. . . .

The Senate Code of Official Conduct contained in Senate Rules 34 through 43 provides very specific standards of conduct on: financial disclosure, gifts, outside earned income and honoraria, conflict of interest, prohibited unofficial office accounts, foreign travel, use of the mailing frank and radio and television studios, political fund activity, employment discrimination, and constituent service. Those Senate rules comprising the Code of Official Conduct are within the exclusive jurisdiction of the Senate Select Committee on Ethics. . . .

Additionally, federal statutes also provide specific standards of conduct in such areas as: conflict of interest, financial disclosure, outside earned income and honoraria, gift acceptance and solicitation, campaign activities, government contracts, foreign travel, and gifts from foreign governments, to name a few. Finally, the United States Constitution contains a prohibition on the acceptance of gifts or emoluments from foreign governments except as permitted by statute. Some federal statutes provide for joint jurisdiction of the ethics committee and the Department of Justice, others are enforced exclusively by the Department of Justice. . . .

Complementing these written standards (i.e., rules and statutes) is a body of unwritten but well-established norms of Senate behavior, violation of which may be deemed "improper conduct reflecting upon the Senate." In other instances the committee, although not declaring conduct to be "improper conduct reflecting upon the Senate" in violation of an unwritten standard, has found that such conduct warranted public criticism, or has stated that it did not condone such conduct.

> "What's troubling about [Senator Christopher] Dodd's scandal isn't so much that it remains unresolved but that it's a textbook example of how scandals in Washington are swept under the rug."

The US Senate Select Committee on Ethics Is Ineffective

Mark Hemingway

Mark Hemingway is a political commentator who has worked for the Weekly Standard, *the* Washington Examiner, National Review Online, USA Today, *and Market News International. In the following viewpoint, he questions the propriety of Senate Banking, Housing, and Urban Affairs Committee chairman Christopher Dodd's receipt of a $75,000 break on a mortgage from subprime mortgage lender Countrywide Financial. Hemingway describes the ways in which members of Congress employ such tactics as denial, stalling, and relying on the ineffectiveness of the Select Committee on Ethics to obstruct corruption investigations, ultimately achieving the desired effect of having the scandal fade from the public's memory.*

As you read, consider the following questions:

1. How much in campaign donations does Hemingway say that Dodd accepted from Countrywide?

2. In Hemingway's judgment, what effect does a politician's use of stalling tactics have on the media coverage of a scandal?

3. How does Hemingway characterize the general reaction of Congress to the alleged unethical behavior of one of its members?

It's been over seven months since it was revealed that Senate Banking[, Housing, and Urban Affairs] Committee chairman Christopher Dodd (D., Conn.) got a sweetheart deal on his Washington, D.C., townhouse directly from Angelo Mozilo, the CEO of troubled subprime mortgage lender Countrywide Financial. Participating in the "Friends of Angelo" program saved Dodd about $75,000 on his mortgage, and raised more than a few eyebrows about whether Dodd should be accepting such hefty gifts from entities he's tasked with overseeing and regulating.

Since the scandal broke last June [in 2008], no action has been taken by the Senate to formally ascertain if Dodd engaged in any wrongdoing. Nor has Dodd tried to clear his name in any way. What's troubling about Dodd's scandal isn't so much that it remains unresolved but that it's a textbook example of how scandals in Washington are swept under the rug. Indeed, Dodd's behavior follows an utterly predictable pattern. Thus, *National Review Online* presents the Christopher Dodd Guide to Managing Political Scandal:

Step 1: Proclaim Your Innocence

Even though an obvious conflict of interest—or even the appearance of one—causes most responsible members of the judiciary to recuse themselves from making legal rulings, very few conflicts of interest are too great to keep members of Congress from writing new laws and regulations—no matter how personally beneficial. In this case, Dodd accepted some $20,000 in campaign donations from Countrywide in addition to receiving a $75,000 mortgage break.

But should a congressman be accused of unethical behavior, the first step in any PR [public relations] offensive is to proclaim his innocence. Whether what he has done is right or wrong is immaterial, as he probably hasn't violated any laws. He'd have to be found in violation of Senate ethics rules, and, well, you'd have better luck playing Powerball.

In this case, Dodd didn't even really try to hide his impropriety. "There ain't much to the story," he told the *Hartford Courant*. Well, if there's *anything* to the story, doesn't the public have a right to know what it is?

Step 2: Promise Exculpatory Evidence but Do Not Keep That Promise

While it's been seven months since the "Friends of Angelo" scandal broke, it's been exactly 188 days since Dodd promised to release all of his pertinent mortgage documents to the public. In July of last year, Dodd told a reporter at the *Courant*: "Yeah, we will [release the mortgage documents] in some time." In September he told the same reporter, "At some point I'll get to it." In late October, he again told the dogged *Courant* staffer, "Not right now. No." That was followed by a statement from his aides saying Dodd "will release them, and he still intends to do that. He intends to do that, not at this time." As recently as this past weekend [in January 2009], he told a crowd at a forum on health care event that "at some point soon we'll do it."

Perhaps Dodd needs to define "soon." Does that mean another six months?

Of course, his stalling here is just the preferred tactic for managing the media coverage of the scandal. "It's hard for people in the media to keep writing stories when there's nothing new to report, which of course they count on. You get through the bad news cycle and there's nothing new to report and people can't keep writing the same thing every day," Melanie Sloan, executive director of Citizens for Responsibility and Ethics in Washington, told *National Review Online.* "The pressure fades and people in Dodd's position know their constituents forget about it."

Step 3: Hide Behind Your Fellow Congressmen

One of the excuses Dodd has given for not releasing his mortgage papers is that they are under review by the Senate Ethics Committee [the Senate Select Committee on Ethics].

"This excuse that the Ethics Committee is looking at them does not preclude him from releasing the documents," Sloan said. "What precludes him from releasing the documents is that there's going to be more stories about him and it might not look so good."

While the press and constituents badger Senator Dodd to account for his mortgage, Dodd insists that he doesn't need to be held publicly accountable because his peers in the Senate are going to make sure that everything is on the up and up.

So when is the Senate Ethics Committee expected to pass judgment on Dodd, you ask?

"Who knows? It's the Ethics Committee. They never say anything and they take forever to do anything. They try and do it as far away from when an issue actually happens so there's a possibility everyone will have forgotten it," Sloan said. "They're not exactly known for their speed or for taking direct action. They give everyone a pass."

The problem isn't just the Ethics Committee, however. It's Congress itself. "Members of Congress never go after each other's ethics, ever. You have to have done something as awful as Bob Packwood [US senator from Oregon who resigned in

"Friends of Angelo"

With Countrywide [Financial]-originated loans serving as fuel and government-sponsored enterprises ("GSEs") Fannie Mae [Federal National Mortgage Association] and Freddie Mac [Federal Home Loan Mortgage Corporation] acting as a furnace, the alliance of the companies created an enormous fire that eventually consumed the American economy. Many of the people in position to reform the GSEs and extinguish the flames before the danger spread were receiving perquisites [privileges] from a VIP loan program operated by Countrywide under the supervision of chairman and CEO [chief executive officer] Angelo Mozilo. These included Fannie Mae chief executive Franklin D. Raines and two senators with legislative jurisdiction over the issues at the heart of the emerging financial crisis—Christopher Dodd and Kent Conrad. . . .

Countrywide's VIP loan program was a tool with which the company built its relationships with members of Congress and congressional staff. . . . Preferential treatment for these potentially influential borrowers, the most important of whom were referred to internally as "Friends of Angelo," was part of an expansive effort by Countrywide to "ingratiate [Countrywide] with people in Washington who might be able to help the company down the road."

Staff Report, US House of Representatives, 111th Congress,
Committee on Oversight and Government Reform,
"Friends of Angelo: Countrywide's Systemic and Successful
Effort to Buy Influence and Block Reform," March 19, 2009.

1995 after allegations of sexual misconduct] or have been convicted of a crime like Stevens," Sloan said. "You have to remember even with [Alaskan Republican senator Ted] Stevens, who was accused of more serious things such as misusing his office for personal gain—even Harry Reid, the Democratic leader, was saying 'He's a long-standing member, we'll wait for the process.'"

"Don't expect them to do anything with Dodd other than to use it as a 'teaching moment' to remind members that the Senate gift rules include loans. I can practically write the letter myself," she said with palpable disgust.

Step 4: Wait Until Everyone Forgets

While the *Hartford Courant*—the biggest paper in his home state—has pursued Dodd's scandal with zeal, the story has already all but vanished from the national media. Initially, many major media outlets, such as the *New York Times*, condemned Dodd's alleged malfeasance; but with no new revelations to report, the story has withered.

That Dodd was questioned again this weekend about his mortgage deals was reported only by the *Courant*. The pressure from the tenacious *Courant* has resulted in disapproval among Dodd's constituents. According to Quinnipiac [a poll that surveys public opinion], last month Dodd registered his lowest approval rating in 14 years. However, with no strong contender for his seat and almost two years until the next election, Dodd is unlikely to be held accountable. That the scandal was ever in the national news at all was only because of Dodd's Banking Committee chairmanship, which made the conflict of interest so brazen it couldn't be ignored. Otherwise it would likely have gone completely unremarked.

Just ask Sen. Kent Conrad (D., N.D.). "It's interesting you only hear about Dodd. Conrad had two mortgages with those people [the 'Friends of Angelo' program]," Sloan said.

And indeed, Senator Conrad's role in the scandal has gone straight down the memory hole. So next time you wonder how members of Congress get away with lining their pockets as they run the country into the ground, remember it's a simple four-step formula—and one that relies on your forgetting you knew it existed in the first place.

> *"Overall, creation of the OCE [Office of Congressional Ethics] has led to much more vigorous enforcement of ethics rules and [has] made the process considerably more transparent."*

The Office of Congressional Ethics Has Potent Political Influence

Citizens for Responsibility and Ethics in Washington (CREW)

Citizens for Responsibility and Ethics in Washington (CREW) advocates the practice of ethics and accountability in government by reporting on officials who betray the public trust in favor of special interests. CREW maintains that the aggressive, transparent methods employed by the Office of Congressional Ethics (OCE) to investigate ethics violations perpetrated by members of the House of Representatives have brought necessary attention to these lawmakers' corrupt dealings. Ironically, CREW observes, OCE's exposure of widespread questionable conduct—particularly involving fund-raising practices—may lead the House to restrict the office's powers of investigation, or perhaps even disband it altogether.

As you read, consider the following questions:

1. According to the viewpoint, what congressional caucus has been especially vocal about limiting the powers of the Office of Congressional Ethics?

2. Why have there been clashes between the Office of Congressional Ethics and the House Ethics Committee, according to CREW?

3. Why does CREW consider the Office of Congressional Ethics a more effective investigative entity than the House Ethics Committee?

Following major Republican scandals involving former majority leader Tom DeLay (R-TX) and lobbyist Jack Abramoff, Democrats took control of the House in 2006, largely because of voter concern over ethics. Following through on her pledge to rid the House of its "culture of corruption," Speaker Nancy Pelosi (D-CA) created the Office of Congressional Ethics (OCE). The OCE—operating with greater transparency than the Ethics Committee [the House Committee on Ethics]—was intended to reinvigorate the moribund ethics process. Although watchdogs welcomed the creation of the OCE, many, including CREW [Citizens for Responsibility and Ethics in Washington], were concerned about whether the office could succeed as structured. The office lacks subpoena power; it can refer matters to the Ethics Committee, but cannot find members broke House rules or federal law, and since the outset, it has had weak political support. Republicans opposed the OCE's creation and many Democrats voted for it only because it was a priority for the Speaker.

Nevertheless, the OCE, which can open investigations based on referrals from the public, has transformed ethics enforcement in the House. So far, it has referred matters involving 13 lawmakers to the Ethics Committee requesting further review. The Ethics Committee dismissed all but two of those cases, finding no wrongdoing. Nevertheless, the OCE has forced the Ethics Committee to directly address matters it might otherwise have ignored, and even when the OCE's referrals have been dismissed, there still have been consequences. Overall, creation of the OCE has led to much more vigorous enforcement of ethics rules and [has] made the process considerably more transparent. Neither of which has made the office very popular on Capitol Hill.

The OCE and the Congressional Black Caucus

The most outspoken critics of the OCE are members of the Congressional Black Caucus (CBC). Although some CBC members did not support the creation of the office in the first place, as the OCE has investigated African American members, CBC members have stepped up their complaints.

Members first took public issue with the office following the OCE's investigation into CBC members' travel to the Caribbean for the Carib News Foundation conference. Following a complaint by the conservative National Legal and Policy Center, the OCE considered whether five CBC members—Del. [Donna] Christensen, Rep. [Carolyn Cheeks] Kilpatrick, Rep. [Donald] Payne, Rep. [Charles] Rangel, and Rep. [Bennie] Thompson—had violated House travel rules by allowing Carib News to pay for their attendance at the organization's conference in November 2008. The OCE found there was a substantial reason to believe the members had accepted expense reimbursement in violation of House rules and referred all five cases to the Ethics Committee. Although the House Ethics Committee cleared five CBC members (including Rep. Yvette Clarke [D-NY], who had not been referred by the OCE) of improperly taking a corporate-funded Caribbean trip, the OCE's reports—noting some of the members had publicly thanked the corporate sponsors and another had underreported the sponsor-paid costs of the trip—still were released. Ultimately, the Ethics Committee admonished only one member, Rep. Rangel, finding—contrary to all evidence—that his staff alone was aware of the corporate sponsorship. As a result of the committee's action, Rep. Rangel was forced to surrender his chairmanship of the House Ways and Means Committee. In part because the Ethics Committee had—after receiving "false and misleading information"—cleared the trip, and in part because CBC members were angry that the OCE released its report, CBC members began to vocally complain about the office and its authority.

Some CBC members also were concerned about the investigation into Rep. [Laura] Richardson—a case illustrative of the OCE's need for subpoena power. The OCE investigated whether Rep. Richardson had received an improper gift after it was revealed that after the congresswoman's home was sold in a foreclosure sale, her lender, Washington Mutual Bank, rescinded the sale. The OCE found there was substantial reason to believe Rep. Richardson had violated House rules by knowingly receiving preferential treatment from the bank. In its report, the OCE noted, however, that it was unable to obtain information from two banks and the foreclosure company involved in the matter because Rep. Richardson refused to allow them to cooperate with the investigation. Further, without offering any explanations, Rep. Richardson herself refused to cooperate with the investigation. Because a determination as to whether Rep. Richardson received preferential treatment required a review of bank documents, the OCE recommended that the Ethics Committee issue subpoenas to Rep. Richardson, the banks and the foreclosure company. Despite e-mail traffic in the government affairs and the communications departments of Washington Mutual about the congresswoman's situation, the Ethics Committee ultimately cleared Rep. Richardson of any wrongdoing.

Bank Ties Raise Ethics Concerns

The OCE also investigated Rep. [Maxine] Waters for failing to reveal her ties to OneUnited Bank when contacting the secretary of the treasury on behalf of the National Bankers Association. In response to Rep. Waters' call, a meeting was granted, but at the meeting and in follow-up conducted by the congresswoman's office, the discussion centered on OneUnited. Rep. Waters' husband had been a board member of the bank from 2004 to 2008 and, at the time of the meeting, held stock in the bank. The OCE referred the matter to the Ethics Committee, finding a substantial reason to believe that Rep. Waters had advocated on behalf of a matter in which she had a personal financial interest. After its own year-long inquiry, an investigative subcommittee of the Ethics Committee agreed and adopted a statement of alleged violation on June 15, 2010. . . .

In May, both Reps. Richardson and Waters met with Speaker Pelosi to complain about their treatment by the OCE. CBC members said investigators' questioning had been abrupt, and complained about the office's lack of minority staffers. One unnamed lawmaker claimed, "There's a dual standard, one for most members and one for African Americans," and argued "this is stacked against you once an accusation is made."

The CBC has engaged in a concerted effort to weaken the OCE. CBC members are supporting a resolution proposed in May by Rep. Marcia Fudge (D-OH) intended to eviscerate the office. The legislation would severely limit the OCE's ability to publicly release its findings; it would prevent the office from referring a matter to the Ethics Committee within 60 days of an election; and most significantly, it would limit the office to investigating only if an individual submits a sworn complaint stating firsthand knowledge of alleged wrongdoing, rather than in response to anonymous complaints or media reports. Rep. Fudge said the new limits are necessary because the "OCE is currently the accuser, judge and jury." Rep. Fudge's role is particularly notable given that her chief of staff, Dawn Kelly Mobley, had been reprimanded by the Ethics Committee for improperly sharing information she obtained as designated counsel to the Ethics Committee during the Carib News investigation.

Majority whip and CBC member Jim Clyburn (D-SC), who is close to the Speaker, has noted, "Several members have raised concerns with the OCE. . . . At some point they will need to be examined and addressed." Personally, Rep. Clyburn believes the office has an "accusatory mentality about every allegation" and agrees the OCE's investigatory process should be changed, saying news stories and headlines shouldn't be sufficient to trigger probes.

Of course, the CBC is not alone in its criticism. Members who have been under investigation and their lawyers also have attempted to discredit the OCE. Cleta Mitchell, a lawyer who defended an unnamed representative against an ethics violation, described the OCE as "a very arrogant, dangerous little outfit," adding, "They are a rogue operation that needs to be shut down." Rep. Sam Graves' (R-MO) attorney, Elliot S. Berke, acknowledged he had encouraged clients not to cooperate with the OCE, in hopes of stymieing the investigation. The tactic was meant to exploit the office's lack of subpoena power. Without that, Rep. Lacy Clay (D-MO) said, "The OCE is like a school-yard bully without any real punch." And, following the OCE's referral of the PMA [Group] matter to the Department of Justice, one Republican lawmaker called the office "out of control" and another said, "I think there's a lot of regrets with having those people [OCE] there."

The OCE Increases Transparency in Congress

In some cases, the Ethics Committee has been forced to release the OCE's reports, which have included records detailing ethically dubious conduct, and provided the public a window into how business is conducted in Washington. For instance, in an investigation into lawmakers' ties to the now defunct PMA Group lobbying firm, the OCE found that two lawmakers—Reps. [Todd] Tiahrt and [Pete] Visclosky—may have tied earmarks to campaign contributions. Although the Ethics Committee found no wrongdoing and dismissed both cases, the OCE referred the matter to the Department of Justice, and its report created additional pressure on congressional leaders to limit earmarks.

Transparency also carried the day in the investigation of Rep. [Nathan] Deal. Following a complaint filed by CREW, the OCE investigated Rep. Deal for using official resources and abusing his position in Congress to bully a Georgia official to benefit his personal business. During the course of the investigation, the OCE found that Rep. Deal had provided inaccurate information on his personal financial disclosure reports. The OCE referred the entire matter to the Ethics Committee for further action. Clearly hoping to avoid a public airing of his ethics violations, Rep. Deal quickly resigned, allegedly to focus on his gubernatorial campaign. Despite his resignation, the OCE released its report, which concluded Rep. Deal had taken "active steps" to preserve a state program "that had generated financial benefit for Representative Deal and his business partner." The Department of Justice is investigating the matter.

There are clear signs that not everyone is basking in the sunlight. Minority leader John Boehner (R-OH) opposed the creation of the OCE in the first place, along with much of his caucus. More recently, he has hinted that the OCE would be dismantled if the Republicans take control of the House. Rep. Boehner said, "It's pretty clear that when this was created, the type of coordination and groundwork that should have been laid was not, and so there are questions that remain about how it works and how effective, in fact, it is."

A Positive Impact on Ethics Oversight

The OCE [Office of Congressional Ethics] isn't perfect, but it has been a pleasant surprise as it has indisputably been a net positive in creating a more transparent and accountable ethics process. At a time when Congress is suffering from very low ratings in the polls, weakening congressional ethics enforcement is exactly the wrong way to rejuvenate its standing with the public. These efforts to drag the process back into the back rooms should be seen for what they are—an act of supreme hubris on the part of Congress and an affront to the American people.

Meredith McGehee,
"Assessing OCE: Separating Rhetoric from Reality,"
Campaign Legal Center Blog, October 8, 2010.
www.clcblog.org.

The OCE and the House Ethics Committee Are at Odds

The Ethics Committee and the OCE have a tense relationship and their spat become public following the OCE's investigation of Rep. Graves. Rep. Graves had ties to a businessman whom he invited to testify before the Committee on Small Business, without revealing the relationship. Absurdly, the Ethics Committee absolved him of any conflict of interest, but even more surprising, when the committee dismissed the case, it criticized the OCE's work as "fundamentally flawed." The committee also accused the OCE of withholding exculpatory evidence in the case, disclosing the names of witnesses, and failing to meet deadlines. The OCE issued a statement of its own, saying it had turned over all evidence to Rep. Graves and otherwise acted appropriately.

The Ethics Committee and the OCE again clashed over the OCE's referral of a case involving whether Rep. [Pete] Stark [D-CA] improperly claimed a tax break for Maryland homeowners. To qualify for the tax break, Maryland law requires the home to be used as the owner's "principal residence," defined as the place where the homeowner regularly resides and designates for voting, obtaining a driver's license, and filing income tax returns. Rep. Stark paid California resident taxes, had a California driver's license, and was registered to vote in California. Despite this evidence, the committee found no wrongdoing in the matter. The Ethics Committee charged that the OCE's investigation of Rep. Stark was inadequate and unfounded because a tax bill that was delivered to Rep. Stark in November or December of 2009 showed that he did not receive the tax break. The OCE responded by pointing out that this tax bill was distributed more than two months after the OCE finished its review, and was not relevant.

Ill will between the Ethics Committee and the OCE remains as Rep. Zoe Lofgren (D-CA), chairwoman of the Ethics Committee, recently blamed the office for "sloppy work" she said has led to unjustified referrals.

The OCE's Effectiveness May Lead to Its Demise

Many lawmakers viewed as inappropriate the OCE's investigation into whether lawmakers traded earmarks for campaign contributions with PMA Group lobbyists. Those concerns have been exacerbated by the OCE's preliminary review of whether members of the House Committee on Financial Services tied campaign contributions to committee votes. In June [2010], the OCE sent letters to lobbyists seeking information about their dealings with eight legislators—five Republicans and three Democrats—regarding their votes on the financial bailout. The OCE was looking at members who held fundraisers within 48 hours of the financial bailout bill or received substantial campaign donations from those with a financial stake in the bill. The probe was focused on whether the timing of the donations created at least the appearance of a conflict of interest. At the end of August, the OCE referred its investigation into three members, Reps. John Campbell (R-CA), Tom Price (R-GA) and Joseph Crowley (D-NY), for further review, but dismissed the cases against the remaining five members.

Expressing a view shared widely on the Hill, campaign finance and ethics lawyer Kenneth Gross, who was involved in the probe, argued, "To pick eight members and say they voted on legislation and political contributions came in around this time is really going places that no regulatory authority has ever gone."

The Exposure of Fund-Raising Practices Threatens the Status Quo

The OCE's investigations into the PMA Group and financial services fund-raising represent a challenge to everyday congressional fund-raising practices, in which members routinely raise money from those with business before them. House precedent, however, clearly establishes that such fund-raising activities are prohibited. As the House Ethics Committee itself noted in a letter of admonition to former House majority leader DeLay, "Under House standards of conduct as set out in Committee publications, a Member may not make a solicitation for campaign or political contributions that is linked with any specific official action taken or to be taken by that Member. In addition, a Member may not accept any contribution that is linked with any specific official action taken or to be taken by that Member." Further, in a related memorandum, the committee warned, "a decent interval of time should be allowed to lapse" between any favor done by a legislator and a campaign contribution "so that neither party will feel that there is a close connection between the two acts."

In addressing the ethics complaint filed against Rep. De-Lay, the committee also stated that a "Member should not make any solicitation that creates even the appearance that campaign contributors will receive or be entitled to either special treatment or special access to the Members in his or her official capacity." The committee found that Rep. DeLay had violated this rule by participating in a fund-raiser with representatives of an energy company just as a House-Senate conference on energy legislation was about to begin.

Reviewing the standards and rules enunciated by the House Ethics Committee in 2004, it is clear that—at least six years ago—the committee took a far dimmer view of the type of conduct the OCE is criticized for investigating today. Perhaps, as members—including those who populate the Ethics Committee—are spending more and more of their time chasing campaign donations, their tolerance for conduct that appears contrary to those rules has increased. It is for this very reason the OCE is so important: Its board, which includes former members of Congress, but who are not now faced with the money chase, can more objectively consider whether activities cross ethical lines. The truth is the OCE simply is doing what the House Ethics Committee either cannot or will not do: enforce ethical standards in the House of Representatives.

> *"Clearly [Representative Maxine Waters] used her influence to come to the aid of a bank in which she and her husband have a big financial stake—an act that the House's conflict of interest rule clearly forbids."*

Dems' Dubious Ethics Tactics the Last Straw?

Donald Lambro

Donald Lambro is chief political correspondent for the Washington Times. *In the following viewpoint, he comments on the charges of ethical misconduct leveled against two members of the US House of Representatives—Rep. Charles Rangel (D-NY) and Rep. Maxine Waters (D-CA)—involving financial malfeasance, misuse of public office, and conflict of interest. Lambro expresses skepticism that the Office of Congressional Ethics will recommend a satisfactory punishment for these scandals, and he argues that it will be up to voters to purge Congress of corrupt members in the 2010 midterm elections.*

As you read, consider the following questions:

1. According to Lambro, what are some conflicts of interest that may have compromised Rep. Charles Rangel's ethical responsibility as chairman of the House Ways and Means Committee?

2. Why does Lambro consider the ethical misconduct of Rep. Maxine Waters more disturbing than that of Rep. Rangel?

3. At the time the viewpoint was written, how did Lambro believe that voters in the 2010 midterm elections would treat Democrats in light of Rangel's and Waters's highly publicized ethics violations?

Two prominent Democrats are facing trial in the House on serious ethics charges less than three months before the voters go to the polls to deliver their midterm verdict.

Both involve severe abuses of power, but one more so than the other as it is entangled in the subprime mortgage debacle that triggered a two-year recession and led to hundreds of billions of dollars in bank bailouts and countless home foreclosures.

New York Rep. Charles Rangel, the once-powerful chairman of the tax-writing House Ways and Means Committee, was forced to step down as a result of 13 ethics charges involving failure to pay taxes, disclose finances, improper political use of a rent-controlled office in New York, and use of his public office to seek millions of dollars in donations from lobbyists and corporations to establish the Charles B. Rangel Center for Public Service at the City College of New York.

In Rangel's case, the House Committee on Standards of Official Conduct, known as the Ethics Committee, has recommended that he be given a "reprimand," the mildest punishment possible. But Rep. Maxine Waters of California, the fiery member of the Congressional Black Caucus, could face a far more severe punishment for seeking a taxpayer bailout for a Boston-based bank, OneUnited, in which her husband, Sidney Williams, served on the board of directors and owned up to $750,000 in stock.

The ethics panel that has been investigating Waters released an 80-page report written last August by the quasi-independent Office of Congressional Ethics that concluded she broke the conflict of interest rule that forbids members from using their influence as a member of Congress for personal financial gain.

OneUnited was in trouble after having lost $50 million in high-risk investments in subprime-backed stocks at federal mortgage giants Fannie Mae and Freddie Mac. At one point, it was seeking nearly $100 million in bailouts from the U.S. Treasury to keep itself afloat.

Federal investigators said the bank had used poor documentation and lending standards, and gave top executives excessive pay and perks that included the use of a $6.4 million beachfront mansion in Santa Monica.

The ethics investigation found that Waters went to then Treasury secretary Henry M. Paulson Jr., asking him to meet with OneUnited executives.

Paulson told investigators later that he believed he was meeting with many minority bankers represented by the National Bankers Association, and was surprised to learn that only OneUnited executives attended. The investigation's preliminary report said "the discussion at the meeting centered on a single bank—OneUnited."

According to the 79-page report by the Office of Congressional Ethics, Waters initially had doubts about the ethical propriety of her action and went to House Banking Committee chairman Barney Frank to get his advice.

"Waters told (Frank) that she was in a predicament because her husband had been involved in the bank, but 'One-

United people' were coming to her for help," the report said. The Massachusetts Democrat told her to "stay out of it," he told investigators.

Waters insists she did nothing wrong by using her influence to set up the meeting with Treasury officials to obtain funding from the Troubled Assets Relief Program (TARP) that eventually handed OneUnited a check for $12.1 million.

But clearly she used her influence to come to the aid of a bank in which she and her husband have a big financial stake—an act that the House's conflict of interest rule clearly forbids.

Rangel's many ethical transgressions are bad enough and led the Ethics Committee to conclude that he broke the "public trust." He, too, said he hadn't done anything improper, and that he had amended House financial disclosure reports he neglected to fill out correctly, paid overdue taxes, and said other members had raised money for centers named after them, as well.

Waters' abuse of her powers and influence as a House member to obtain special treatment for OneUnited Bank is arguably worse. "This sure has an unethical whiff to it," the *Washington Post* said in an editorial Tuesday in a classic bit of understatement.

Both ethics scandals come at a time when public disapproval of the Democratic Congress is at an all-time high. More than 80 House seats are in play in November—mostly held by Democrats—and Republicans need only 39 of them to take control of the now-aptly named "lower chamber."

But let's face it, this election is going to be a midterm referendum on the Obama administration and its handling of a jobless recovery, which remains weak and mediocre, and the legislative excesses of the Democratic Congress, i.e., health care reform, the budget deficit, business regulations and plans to raise taxes in a weak economy at the end of this year.

But it will also be about ethics and honesty in the Capitol, and the trials of Rangel and Waters will give voters two additional reasons to conclude that the Democrats are not hosting "the most ethical Congress in history."

"*There is one way that the ethics process has improved since 2006: the introduction of the Office of Congressional Ethics (OCE).*"

The Office of Congressional Ethics Has Improved Oversight

Paul Blumenthal

Paul Blumenthal is a contributor to the Huffington Post. *Previously, he served as a senior writer for the Sunlight Foundation. In the following viewpoint, he questions whether or not the trials of Rep. Charles Rangel (D-NY) and Rep. Maxine Waters (D-CA) indicate that the ethical review process adequately deters lawmakers from engaging in misconduct. Blumenthal concludes that since 2007 the Office of Congressional Ethics (OCE) has strengthened the oversight of congressional members' ethical behavior despite some lawmakers' concerted efforts to undermine the office's authority or obstruct its investigations.*

As you read, consider the following questions:

1. What does Blumenthal state has been the most tangible improvement in the congressional ethical review process since 2006?

2. According to Blumenthal, what new tactic are lawmakers using to obstruct or delay judgment during the ethical review process?

3. In Blumenthal's judgment, have lawmakers enthusiastically supported the Office of Congressional Ethics?

Chris Van Hollen, the House Democrat's campaign chief, recently stated that the upcoming ethics trials of Reps. Charlie Rangel and Maxine Waters prove that the ethics process has been strengthened under the watch of the majority Democrats. I'm not so sure that that's the case.

If we take a walk back through time, we'll see that the Ethics Committee [the House Committee on Ethics] was plenty busy in the nineties and even during the dark days of the early to mid aughts.

Over the course of ten years during the Republican majority, the committee issued five admonishments (three to Rep. Tom DeLay), two letters of reproval, one sanction and one expulsion. Of course, there were also numerous issues that the committee failed to cover including the Jack Abramoff scandal [a 1990s lobbying scandal] and the Duke Cunningham scandal [a bribery, fraud, and tax evasion scandal].

Lawmakers Resist Ethics Process

What appears to make the recent spate of ethics flare-ups notable is that the members involved are refusing to accept a lesser punishment by publicly accepting guilt and responsibility. Both Rangel and Waters have clearly been offered deals to accept lesser penalties in lieu of a trial. In 2004, Tom DeLay accepted committee admonishments and never went to trial. It's clear that what is operating differently at this stage of the ethics process is the obstinance of the lawmakers involved.

Despite that, there is one way that the ethics process has improved since 2006: the introduction of the Office of Congressional Ethics (OCE). The creation of OCE, a body created out of compromise in the Honest Leadership and Open Government Act of 2007, has enabled a less corruptible body to review ethics complaints with more freedom and less clubbiness than the traditional Ethics Committee. The Waters charges began as an OCE investigation and were referred to the Ethics Committee.

Certainly, this counts as an improvement that has happened under the watch of the Democrats. The fact that two lawmakers refused to accept deals for lesser punishments and are pushing for public trials, not so much.

If Van Hollen wants to take credit for something else, he can also point out that the current majority has followed a simple dictate: do no harm. The majority Democrats have not yet struck out to dismantle or neuter the ethics process, particularly OCE, despite pressure coming from both sides of the aisle.

Both Parties Obstruct Ethics Review

The Congressional Black Caucus (CBC) and Republican minority leader John Boehner have both been critical of the independent ethics office. If lawmakers want to truly maintain and expand upon a more just and credible ethics process, they need to retain OCE as it is or increase its authority.

In 2005, after majority leader DeLay received three admonishments from the committee, he moved to purge the committee of its members and change the way in which the committee ran investigations. The move was widely panned and the majority Republicans would have to walk back the changes in the coming months.

Neither the Democrats, if they retain the majority, nor the Republicans, if they win back control, should move to dismantle the ethics process by reducing the role of the independent OCE. The rhetoric coming from the CBC and minority leader Boehner are not encouraging. Hopefully they won't follow DeLay's lead and neuter the ethics process again.

Ethics Abuses Abound in Congress

I've included a quick summary of actions taken by the Ethics Committee since 1996 below:

- 1996: The Ethics Committee dismissed charges that Rep. Tom DeLay linked campaign contributions to his official actions and made improper favors to his brother, a lobbyist. The Ethics Committee also sanctioned Rep. Bud Shuster for serious official misconduct in dealings with his former chief of staff turned lobbyist.

- 1997: The committee gave Speaker of the House Newt Gingrich a letter of reproval for violating tax laws and providing false information to the committee. The committee also fined Gingrich $300,000, the largest fined issued by the committee in its history. Later in the year, the committee brought a six-count statement of alleged violations against Rep. Jay Kim after he plead guilty to three misdemeanor charges of accepting illegal campaign contributions. The charges were dropped as Kim had lost his primary and the committee no longer held jurisdiction.

- 1999: The committee dismissed charges against Rep. Corrine Brown, but stated that the congresswoman had used "poor judgment." Rep. Earl Hilliard received a letter of reproval after a three-count statement of alleged violations was brought against him for making improper loans to his campaign committee, failing to properly file financial disclosure forms and making payments from his campaign to nonprofits and companies connected to him.

- 2001: The committee voted to expel Rep. Jim Traficant after he was found guilty of bribery, racketeering, tax evasion and many other laws. The full House of Representatives voted to expel Traficant in 2002. The committee also dismissed claims against Rep. Steve Buyer.

- 2004: The committee admonished three members, Reps. Tom DeLay, Candice Miller and Nick Smith, for their actions during the vote on the Medicare Prescription Drug, Improvement and Modernization Act. DeLay also received two separate admonishments for other violations of laws and House ethics rules.

- 2006: The committee dismissed complaints against Jeffrey Shockey, the deputy chief of staff to Rep. Jerry Lewis. Rep. John Conyers was scolded by the committee for letting his congressional staff do campaign work. The committee also settled a long-running dispute by ruling that Rep. Jim McDermott had violated the spirit of the House by leaking information related to the ethics investigation of then Speaker Gingrich to the press.

- 2007: Former Reps. Tom Feeney and Curt Weldon were ordered to pay for travel that they accepted in violation of House rules. Feeney agreed to pay, but it is unclear whether the committee has jurisdiction to force Weldon to pay.

- 2010: The committee brought a thirteen-count statement of alleged violations against Rep. Charlie Rangel for a variety of violations of House rules. That case will be adjudicated. The committee brought a state of alleged violations against Rep. Maxine Waters, who will also take the case to the adjudication phase. Rangel was also admonished separately for accepting corporate-paid travel. The committee also cleared the following members on a variety of charges: Reps. Pete Stark, Pete Visclosky, Bill Young, Norm Dicks, John Murtha, Marcy Kaptur, Todd Tiahrt, James Moran, Bennie Thompson, Yvette Clarke, Carolyn Cheeks Kilpatrick and Del. Donna Christensen.

> "The committee charged with policing the entire House seemed at times unable to enforce the rules of its own panel."

The House Ethics Committee Has Failed to Improve Ethics Oversight

John Bresnahan

John Bresnahan is a senior congressional reporter for Politico. In the following viewpoint, he comments on a controversy involving the House Committee on Ethics, in which two staffers allegedly improperly passed sensitive information about investigations into the affairs of Reps. Charles Rangel (D-NY) and Maxine Waters (D-CA) to Republican members on the panel. Bresnahan maintains that confidential e-mails and memos acquired by Politico reveal that the Ethics Committee is rife with partisanship, turf wars, and unprofessional conduct. Bresnahan relates details of the committee's involvement in the investigations of Rangel and Waters as well as illustrates that the committee has mishandled its role and responsibilities.

As you read, consider the following questions:

1. According to Bresnahan, what actions committed by House Ethics Committee staffers compromised the integrity of investigations into the alleged unethical conduct of Reps. Charles Rangel and Maxine Waters?

2. How does Bresnahan characterize the working relationship of House Ethics Committee members based on a survey of supposedly confidential internal e-mails and memos?

3. In Bresnahan's judgment, do these confidential documents indicate that the House Ethics Committee maintains an appropriate level of objectivity in its investigations?

The former staff director of the House Ethics Committee [the House Committee on Ethics] accused two top committee lawyers last year [in 2010] of secretly communicating with Republicans on the panel regarding the investigations of Democratic Reps. Maxine Waters and Charles Rangel, raising concerns over whether the long-running inquiries were compromised by key staffers, according to internal committee documents obtained by Politico.

Blake Chisam, the former staff director, wrote in a late 2010 memo to then chairwoman Zoe Lofgren (D-Calif.) that attorneys Morgan Kim and Stacy Sovereign improperly shared information in the Rangel case with Republicans on the committee—a move that "would have so tainted the proceedings that there would have been no option but to move to dismiss." The Ethics Committee places strict limits on the sharing of evidence during "trials" for lawmakers; committee members act as prosecutors and lawmakers play the role of a jury.

While the Rangel case is over—he was censured by the full House in December 2010—the allegations about Kim and

Sovereign could have a major impact as the Ethics Committee prepares to meet on the Waters case early this week [in July 2011].

The Committee's Handling of Ethics Cases Is Questioned

Kim, who was the lead attorney on the investigation into Waters's finances, and Sovereign were suspended from their jobs late last year amid questions about their handling of the case. In addition, Waters's case was effectively put on hold.

Now Waters is using the allegations about staff wrongdoing to ask for her case to be dismissed altogether. Some ethics experts agree and believe this could derail the Waters case or create the need for the Ethics Committee to hire an independent counsel to take over the matter.

Kim and Sovereign, former federal prosecutors, no longer work on the Ethics Committee.

Richard Sauber, an attorney for Kim and Sovereign, rejected Chisam's assessment of his clients' actions, countering that Kim and Sovereign "were used as scapegoats by the chief of staff [Chisam] and former [chairwoman Lofgren] to cover up the implosion inside the committee due to partisan infighting" among committee members.

Chisam's memo is among hundreds of pages of confidential Ethics Committee e-mails, memos and notes obtained by Politico involving the high-profile investigations into Waters and Rangel that for the first time lay out the details of the allegations surrounding the suspensions of Kim and Sovereign.

Documents Suggest Dysfunction on the Ethics Committee

The documents also paint a picture of a committee—evenly divided between the two parties—riven with partisan plots, petty jealousies and competing agendas. Indeed, the commit-

Copyright © 2010, by Pat Bagley and CagleCartoons.com.

tee charged with policing the entire House seemed at times unable to enforce the rules of its own panel.

The Ethics Committee would not comment for this [viewpoint].

In a series of memos to Lofgren, Chisam revealed a wide range of problems inside the secretive, powerful committee. Chisam, who also declined to comment, left the Ethics Committee in January for a job in a private law firm.

For example, Rep. Jo Bonner (R-Ala.), former ranking member of the Ethics Committee, and at least one Bonner aide not authorized to access confidential panel materials, received e-mails and other information from Kim and Sovereign on the Rangel and Waters cases, Chisam said in his memo. Bonner is now chairman of the Ethics Committee.

Texas Rep. Mike McCaul, the top Republican on the special panel overseeing the Rangel trial, also received material from Kim regarding the case, according to Chisam's memo. As professional, nonpartisan staff members, Kim and Sovereign were barred from unapproved contact with certain Ethics Committee members during portions of cases, including the Rangel trial.

"They have engaged in impermissible ex parte communication with Republican staff and members of the committee," Chisam said of Kim and Sovereign in a separate memo in December that he sent to Lofgren.

Partisan Meddling Complicates Investigation

According to Ethics Committee documents prepared in the wake of their suspension, Chisam believed Kim and Sovereign were improperly passing information to Republicans on the Ethics Committee in order to hurt Rangel and Waters. Chisam also accused Sovereign of engaging in "insubordinate behavior and factual misrepresentations" and said they "affirmatively misled" him and Ethics Committee members about the status of the Waters probe.

In a separate set of notes prepared for Lofgren in late 2010, Chisam said Kim and Sovereign failed to provide Waters and her defense team with all the materials the Ethics Committee uncovered as required under panel rules. Chisam also said the two improperly accessed other Ethics Committee staffers' computers for information.

Chisam, in a note to Lofgren, "recommended that [Kim and Sovereign] be separated from their service on the committee." Chisam conducted a review into the pair's alleged actions, including checking their e-mail records on Ethics Committee computers, after they were suspended.

While most of the Ethics Committee documents obtained by Politico focus on the problems with how Kim and Sovereign handled the Rangel and Waters cases, there were some counter-accusations against Chisam.

Kim and Sovereign, in e-mails between themselves and Republicans on the Ethics Committee, contend that Chisam withheld evidence against Rangel in advance of his trial, including accusations that Rangel solicited millions of dollars from insurance giant AIG for the Charles B. Rangel Center for Public Service.

They also privately accused Chisam, who worked for Lofgren's personal office before being hired to run the Ethics Committee, of secretly trying to protect Democrats. The Ethics Committee files obtained by Politico—which don't contain the entire record of the cases—don't contain evidence that Chisam interfered in the Waters and Rangel cases.

The Ethics Committee Is Under Fire from Delays

Those allegations, laid out in extensive detail in memos, notes and e-mail files from the panel, could prove a nightmare for the Ethics Committee, which is already under fire over its failure to move forward on the Waters case nearly eight months after postponing a trial for the California Democrat.

Kim and Sovereign were placed on "paid administrative leave" by Lofgren in mid-November following an intense, behind-the-scenes battle with Bonner, a showdown that included a lockout of committee offices.

Bonner, at the time, refused to allow Lofgren and Chisam to fire the two staffers outright, although Democrats later prevented them from returning to the committee when Bonner tried to hire them for the 112th Congress. Kim has since moved to the Natural Resources Committee, while Sovereign has left Capitol Hill.

In a letter that Bonner sent to Ethics Committee members in March, the Alabama Republican said Kim and Sovereign had "acted appropriately and consistent with the highest ethical standards." Bonner said he consulted with all other members of the Ethics Committee before issuing his letter clearing Kim and Sovereign.

It's unclear how the Ethics Committee will settle the Waters case.

Concerns About Objectivity Stymie Process

Waters has been charged with three ethics violations for allegedly improperly intervening on behalf of a minority-owned bank where her husband owned more than $350,000 in stock during the 2008 financial crisis. Waters has denied the charges, but her case has been on hold since last November, when the Ethics Committee postponed the trial after claiming new evidence was uncovered.

Waters has waged a bitter legal struggle against the Ethics Committee charges, which were made public last summer. Her attorneys have challenged the standards used for deciding whether she broke House rules.

"I have long since lost faith in the committee's ability to be fair and transparent," Waters said in a statement to Politico after learning of the Chisam memos. "If true, these accusations fly in the face of objectivity and should concern every member of the House. Even more troubling is the committee's refusal of my and numerous ethics watchdogs' requests to investigate their own misconduct. Given what appears to be politically motivated and gross misconduct by the committee, the committee must immediately conclude this seemingly manufactured case."

These latest revelations could also reopen the controversy surrounding Rangel, who was found guilty of 11 ethics violations tied to his personal finances, including improperly soliciting donations for his center for public service at the City College of New York. Rangel was censured by the House last December, the first time any member has faced such a punishment in nearly three decades.

That issue became moot when Rangel—whose lawyers quit just weeks before the trial despite the $2 million Rangel spent on his defense—refused to participate in the proceedings and stalked out. The special subcommittee then quickly found Rangel guilty on 11 charges and dismissed two others.

Kim, in a Nov. 15, 2010, document prepared for her own use, supplied at least one possible question to Republicans serving on the Rangel jury, a query she called "The nuclear option—don't ask unless things go bad." This referred to allegations that Rangel, former chairman of the powerful House Ways and Means Committee, sought millions of dollars in contributions from insurance giant AIG for the Rangel center when the company had legislation before Rangel's committee, a potential ethical, or even criminal, violation. Rangel was never charged with such an improper quid pro quo [favor granted in exchange for something else].

> "Right-wing legal organizations are using the Office of Congressional Ethics (OCE) . . . to target black members of Congress."

Congressional Ethics Oversight Appears to Be Racially Biased

G. Derek Musgrove

G. Derek Musgrove is a professor of history at the University of the District of Columbia and the author of Rumor, Repression, and Racial Politics: How the Harassment of Black Elected Officials Shaped Post-Civil Rights America. *In the following viewpoint, he asserts that black lawmakers in the US House of Representatives are being targeted more than their white peers for alleged ethics violations. In Musgrove's opinion, several conservative legal groups are filing questionable ethics complaints against black lawmakers with the Office of Congressional Ethics (OCE) in a partisan effort to undermine the integrity of the Democratic Party as a whole.*

As you read, consider the following questions:

1. According to Musgrove, what percentage of black members of Congress are investigated for ethics violations versus their white counterparts?

2. Why does Musgrove believe that conservative legal organizations are targeting black members of Congress for unethical conduct?

3. What kinds of reforms to the Office of Congressional Ethics does Musgrove propose to prevent partisan meddling in investigations?

An anonymous member of the Congressional Black Caucus charged that black lawmakers are being targeted in ethics investigations. Some say the whistle-blower is playing the race card. But that nameless CBC member is right.

Recently, an anonymous member of the Congressional Black Caucus (CBC) charged that the ethics investigations of Representatives Charlie Rangel (D-N.Y.) and Maxine Waters (D-Calif.) demonstrate that black lawmakers face disproportionate levels of ethical investigation than their white colleagues.

Right-wing pundits, like Bernie Goldberg, immediately cried foul, arguing that the assertion constituted "playing the race card"—at this point, an old and tired right-wing response to African Americans' identification of racial disparities. Good government watchdogs, like Meredith McGehee of the Campaign Legal Center, argued that the investigations aren't racially biased. When constituents don't hold an elected official accountable—when they've held that position for years and years virtually uncontested—they are more likely to be vulnerable to the temptations of unethical behavior, a claim for which she offered no proof.

But that nameless CBC member is correct.

A Disproportionate Focus on
Black Representatives

Since 2008 the House Ethics Committee [the House Committee on Ethics] has devoted a disproportionate amount of its time to cases involving black members of Congress. Of the 42 members of the CBC in the House of Representatives, seven, or 16.5 percent, have been investigated by the Ethics Committee in the past two years. Though the committee does not release information about whom it is investigating unless formal charges are brought, it can safely be argued that no comparable percentage of white members have faced investigation. When we add up the published reports of cases, like the investigations of Rep. Eric Massa and the PMA Group [a now defunct lobbying firm accused of congressional corruption], the number of white members investigated in the past two years appears to be more like 35, or just shy of 9 percent.

These figures, in and of themselves, do not suggest a sinister intent on the part of ethics investigators. If members of the CBC disproportionately engage in graft, they should be disproportionately investigated by the Ethics Committee. But there is no evidence that members of the CBC disproportionately engage in graft. There is evidence, however, that right-wing legal organizations are using the Office of Congressional Ethics (OCE), which refers cases to the Ethics Committee, to target black members of Congress.

All but one of the investigations of black members of the House of Representatives before the Ethics Committee in the past two years were begun based on claims filed by right-wing legal groups. In 2008 the National Legal and Policy Center—a self-described "conservative watchdog organization" that has a long and disturbing history of filing ethics complaints against liberal Democrats, particularly black Democrats, and ignoring the ethically questionable actions of conservative Republicans—filed the initial claim in five of the seven investigations.

In 2009 the Landmark Legal Foundation, an anti-labor conservative legal group, asked the Ethics Committee to investigate John Conyers (D-Mich.).

In short, the disproportionate number of Ethics Committee investigations of members of the CBC is the product of several right-wing legal groups' efforts to use the OCE to attack the Democratic Party by targeting its most loyal constituency. Republicans have found blacks a particularly attractive target in recent years because white Democrats refuse to defend them, perhaps out of fear that doing so will alienate white Democratic voters. (Think Jeremiah Wright, ACORN, the New Black Panther Party and Shirley Sherrod: all fabricated controversies generated and pushed by right-wing media and political organizations.)

Partisan Agendas Must Be Removed from the Process

Thus, the recent spate of Ethics Committee investigations of black members of Congress is not really about those black members. It is a product of the partisan warfare that has engulfed Washington, D.C., in the last several decades, a partisan warfare in which Republicans have freely used race to attack Democrats.

What should be done about it? How can lawmakers be held accountable in a time when both political parties use charges of ethical impropriety as political weapons? First, Democrats should allow the ethics process to run its course. A number of freshman Democrats in swing districts—including Representatives Michael Arcuri (D-N.Y.), Debbie Halvorson (D-Ill.), Paul Hodes (D-N.H.), Mary Jo Kilroy (D-Ohio), Ann Kirkpatrick (D-Ariz.) Walter Minnick (D-Idaho), Zack Space (D-Ohio), Betty Sutton (D-Ohio) and John Yarmuth (D-Ky.)—have called for Rangel to resign, apparently hoping that so doing will shield them from Republican efforts, already under way, to link them to the Harlem lawmaker in the midterm

Are Ethics Investigations Racially Motivated?

It is a grave accusation: Could the congressional ethics process, ostensibly safeguarded by professional staff members and by a bipartisan structure that allows nothing to move forward unless Democrats and Republicans agree, be singling out African Americans?

Other explanations are possible. Perhaps more ethical issues arise within the black caucus than within the House as a whole. Many of its members occupy safe seats, after all, and have been in Washington for decades. Maybe some of them grew too comfortable or insulated, and they failed to track changing ethics standards.

Or maybe they're disproportionately the victims of an investigation process that relies heavily on outside information from watchdog groups with their own agendas, or on big-city media prone to examining politicians in their urban backyards. Or maybe their white counterparts are quicker to retain high-priced counsel to make ethics inquiries disappear before they ever become public or have quickly resigned rather than face a probe.

Shane Goldmacher, "Disparate Impact:
Black Lawmakers and Ethics Investigations,"
National Journal, *March 3, 2012.*

elections. They miss the point. These investigations are not about the individual members but about partisan warfare. Republicans will use the Rangel and Waters cases as electoral issues, whether or not Democrats jump the gun and oust these members before they have had a chance to defend themselves.

Second, Democrats (and I say Democrats because Republicans are generating and benefiting from the cases discussed here) need to reform the OCE to make it less susceptible to abuse. Rep. Marcia Fudge (D-Ohio) has introduced legislation, cosponsored by 19 members of the CBC, that would restrict disclosure of investigations by the OCE and require that body to obtain a sworn complaint from a citizen with personal knowledge of the alleged wrongdoing before initiating a probe. Though lambasted by critics as an attempt to weaken the OCE, the legislation would actually make it harder for partisan groups to use the panel to attack their political opposition. Hopefully, Democrats will overcome the racial politics of the Rangel and Waters investigations to implement policies that will ensure a robust ethics process that is less vulnerable to abuse.

> *"No one is above the law. And, for that matter, it's obvious that ethical lapses in judgment know no party label— much less skin color."*

Congressional Ethics Oversight Is Not Racially Biased

Armstrong Williams

Armstrong Williams is a conservative columnist and talk show host. In the following viewpoint, he maintains that Reps. Charles Rangel (D-NY) and Maxine Waters (D-CA) are being investigated by the House Committee on Ethics because they got caught engaging in unethical behavior, not because they are black. Williams observes that corruption scandals have ensnared both white and black—as well as Republican and Democratic—Congress members. He argues that it is up to American voters to scrutinize a representative's ethics during an election and vote the politician out of office if he or she betrays the public trust.

Armstrong Williams, "Ethics Charges Offer Democrats No Way Out in November," *Washington Times*, September 19, 2010. www.washingtontimes.com. Copyright © 2010 The Washington Times LLC. This reprint does not constitute or imply any endorsement or sponsorship of any product, service, company or organization. License #31219.

As you read, consider the following questions:

1. How does Williams characterize both the Republican and Democratic leaders' response to unethical conduct among members of their respective political parties?

2. Why is Williams suspicious of allegations of racism when corruption charges are leveled at black members of Congress?

3. In Williams's opinion, how can American voters help reduce the amount of corruption in Congress?

Like many, I like to spend my summer months catching up on some good books and vacationing in Europe. Only this year [2010], I've stopped reading fiction.

Why bother when real life is so much more interesting? In fact, I think I'll stop reading books altogether for the next several weeks. All I need are the latest editions of the *Hill* and the *Washington Times* to follow the scintillating scandals that have totally rocked Democratic Reps. Charles B. Rangel of New York and Maxine Waters of California. I know fiction writers are green with envy with these developing story lines.

The latest developments surrounding the Waters and Rangel cases have both looking like they will spend 2011 in retirement; perhaps even in the pokey if there's another shoe that has yet to fall.

Both claim their innocence, with Mr. Rangel defiantly telling supporters and whoever else will listen at his annual mega-birthday bash earlier this year that he will fight these allegations with every fiber of his being.

Leadership Is Lacking in Congress

Has anyone seen this summer movie before? I have. Try 2006 when Republicans such as Reps. Rick Renzi, Richard W. Pombo, Mark Foley and others lined up to the microphones to declare their innocence. Instead of summarily removing them from office (or at least asking them to step down from running that year), Republican leaders whistled in the other direction, refusing to set an example. Rep. John Boehner of Ohio publicly asked Mr. Renzi to step down. Mr. Pombo and Mr. Foley were not publicly asked to resign.

And here we are, barely four years later, and after publicly calling out the Republicans for their ethical filth, House Speaker Nancy Pelosi spends her mornings at the Four Seasons whistling away the day, hoping Mr. Rangel and Mrs. Waters figure out this mess before it spills onto her hair. Her best solution so far? Moving the hearings until after the November elections. Apparently "draining the swamp" of corruption means covering the marsh with a tarp and pretending it's a meadow.

And then (cue the music) allegations of racism fill the political theater. "You're going after these members only because they're black," come the cries. This was a predictable, if not humdrum, response. After all, if mere opposition to the Democrats' health care overhaul made white Americans racist; if mere opposition to tax increases by white Americans makes them necessarily racist; if merely believing that affirmative action is wrong makes white Americans racist, then of course we expected that to charge a black public official with unethical, or especially illegal, activity would also be dismissed as racism. The racism charge has been so haphazardly . . . leveled at anyone who opposes the left's agenda that had skin color not come up in the Rangel and Waters cases, I might have had to look out the window to see if the world was coming to an end.

But there's color at stake here all right. The color green. The allure of the money pulled these two titans from the mountain. After decades of "doing right" and "following the rules," these two got clumsy. They excused their actions in the name of a higher purpose. For Mr. Rangel, it was a center, library or some other building with his name on it. Not paying

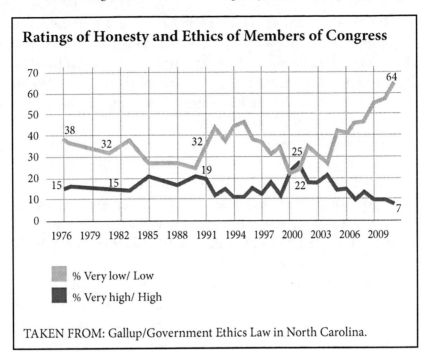

Ratings of Honesty and Ethics of Members of Congress

TAKEN FROM: Gallup/Government Ethics Law in North Carolina.

taxes on properties in the Dominican Republic when you're the chairman of the House tax-writing panel? A minor oversight. Besides, I don't speak the language.

But he does know how to say "dollars" in Spanish.

Corruption Is Color-Blind

The only bias on display in these investigations would be if the Ethics Committee [the House Committee on Ethics] looked the other way because Mr. Rangel and Mrs. Waters were black. No one is above the law. And, for that matter, it's obvious that ethical lapses in judgment know no party label— much less skin color.

A look back at the past decade in Washington politics ought to teach Americans an important lesson about corruption. It's simple. Both sides have their bad apples. Americans threw out the Republican bums in 2006, hoping that replacing them with Democrats would usher in an era of political purity.

But power corrupts, as the saying goes, and because absolute power corrupts absolutely, we established a system of checks and balances—and, most important, we established elections to allow Americans to purge Washington and their statehouses when the leaders forget who they are and what good governance really is all about.

Do the recent revelations of excess and abuse by several Democratic members of Congress mean that the Democratic Party itself is corrupt, and did the few Republicans who abused their positions when they were in power represent Republicans at large? Or even more narrowly that Americans now need to throw all the bums out in Washington and replace them with Republicans?

While it would certainly serve my own self-interest as a conservative to argue that yes, this means we need to get rid of all Democrats, what it really means is that Americans need to look more closely at the individual members who represent them and ask themselves, "Is he or she on the level? Does my representative in Congress truly represent my needs, or is he or she there only to serve his or her own self-interest?"

Politics and Corruption Go Hand in Hand

No matter who is in charge in Washington, corrupt individuals will surface. It's human nature. It's the cycle of political life. Political corruption doesn't check itself at any party door.

But Americans are still likely to hold the Democratic Party responsible for a few of its members' ethics violations, regardless of their skin color. And that's fine by this conservative. I'm in no rush to show the Democrats a way out of this mess.

Periodical and Internet Sources Bibliography

The following articles have been selected to supplement the diverse views presented in this chapter.

Earl "Skip" Cooper "Congresswoman Maxine Waters: Advocating as Always for the Underrepresented," *Black Business News*, August 2010.

Susan Crabtree "Small Office Has Big Job as Monitor of Ethics in the House," *Washington Times*, March 19, 2012.

Eric Lipton "Watt, Once Its Target, Wants Ethics Office's Budget Cut," *New York Times*, July 21, 2011.

Meredith McGehee "An Ethics Process Badly in Need of Reform," *The Hill's Congress Blog*, July 22, 2011. http://thehill.com.

National Legal and Policy Center "Countrywide Probe Is Chance for Ethics Committee to Do 'Something Significant,'" December 21, 2011. http://nlpc.org.

Norman Ornstein "Ethics Committee's Shortcomings on Display," *Roll Call*, July 20, 2011.

Manu Raju and John Bresnahan "Ethics Committee: John Ensign Spun 'Web of Deceit,'" Politico.com, May 12, 2011.

John Reiniers "House Ethics Panel—Fuel for Politics and Media," *Hernando Today*, February 27, 2012.

Sylvia A. Smith "Ethics Upgrade Cleaning House," *Journal Gazette* (Fort Wayne, IN), October 3, 2010.

Jacob R. Straus "Enforcement of Congressional Rules of Conduct: An Historical Overview," Congressional Research Service, June 14, 2011.

OPPOSING
VIEWPOINTS®
SERIES

CHAPTER 2

What Impact Do Congressional Ethics Have on Social and Political Issues?

Chapter Preface

As it does with so many other matters related to the function of the federal government, the US Constitution only provides broad guidelines for establishing a code of ethical conduct in the House of Representatives and the Senate. Article I, Section 5 of the Constitution states, "Each House may determine its rules of proceeding, punish its Members for disorderly behavior, and, with the concurrence of two-thirds, expel a Member." What the framers of the Constitution considered "disorderly behavior" is not exactly clear, but the instructions reflect a desire to avoid the often unruly proceedings found in the British parliamentary system upon which elements of the US government are based. As a result, many believe that the reference to "disorderly behavior" in the Constitution merely addresses the propriety of a Congress member's ethical actions within the confines of the legislative body and does not necessarily assume any authority to regulate the member's conduct outside of the Capitol. Further, the restrictive means by which it takes to expel a member of Congress for disruptive activity—i.e., a two-thirds vote of the legislative body as opposed to a simple majority—underscores the expectation that a careful process of debate and deliberation must accompany any effort to remove a duly elected official from either the House or the Senate.

Despite the generality with which the Constitution addresses ethical behavior in Congress, the founding fathers of the United States recognized that institutional safeguards needed to be implemented in order to control corruption and the abuse of power. In "Federalist No. 51"—part of a series of articles written between 1787 and 1788 by James Madison, Alexander Hamilton, and John Jay to promote the ratification of the Constitution—Madison writes, "If men were angels, no government would be necessary. If angels were to govern men, neither external nor internal controls on government would be necessary. In framing a government which is to be administered by men over men, the great difficulty lies in this: You must first enable the government to control the governed; and in the next place oblige it to control itself." The solution that the framers of the Constitution came up with was to design an elaborate system of checks and balances and separation of powers that prevented any one person or political faction from accumulating too much power within the federal government. However, with respect to monitoring the integrity of elected officials, the founding fathers saw fit to leave the details of creating a system of ethical oversight to the members of the two legislative houses themselves.

Nearly two hundred years passed before Congress adopted a formal process of investigating and disciplining ethical misconduct among its members. In 1964 the US Senate created what is currently known as the Senate Select Committee on Ethics in response to a series of political corruption scandals that exposed abuses of power, conflicts of interest, and many other ethical improprieties perpetrated by members of the legislative body. The House of Representatives followed suit in 1967, founding what is today known as the House Committee on Ethics to enforce, investigate, and discipline any ethics violations committed by lawmakers in that legislative body. In the wake of a series of highly publicized and embarrassing political scandals in the 2000s, the House decided to fortify its ethics oversight process. To this end, it authorized the creation of an independent, nonpartisan agency, entitled the Office of Congressional Ethics (OCE) in 2008. While the OCE has caused a fair degree of consternation among many members of the House chiefly due to its aggressive methods of investigation, both the national media and government watchdog groups have praised the agency for helping to increase the transparency and openness surrounding many of the deliberately secretive practices that occur in the US Congress.

The constitutional basis for ethical and moral behavior in Congress and the impact of such behavior on the legislative process are just some of the issues addressed in the following chapter. Other viewpoints explore the effect of legislative actions on such issues as climate change and biotechnology, and how unethical behavior by members of Congress affects the political process.

> "Because the impacts of climate change are so potentially devastatingly catastrophic to millions of poor people around the world, willful ignorance of climate change causation must be understood to be deeply, ethically reprehensible."

Congressional Lapses in Ethics on Climate Change Can Have Disastrous Environmental Effects

Donald A. Brown

Donald A. Brown is an associate professor of environmental ethics, science, and law at Pennsylvania State University. In the following viewpoint, he describes congressional hearings that sought to discredit the significance of global warming as a travesty in ethical judgment. Brown argues that several Republican Congress members displayed willful ignorance in refusing to accept the mounting scientific evidence of climate change. He concludes that such denial constitutes a serious breach of ethics that not only threatens the well-being of the environment but also affects the lives of millions of people who will suffer from the catastrophic effects of climate change.

As you read, consider the following questions:

1. In Brown's judgment, did Republican lawmakers invite an impartial panel of witnesses to testify on climate change during congressional hearings on the subject?

2. According to Brown, who was the first philosopher to explain the ethical dimensions of willful ignorance?

3. What role does Brown maintain that the National Academy of Sciences is supposed to play in its dealings with Congress?

In an April 4, 2011, *New York Times* op-ed entitled "The Truth, Still Inconvenient," Paul Krugman charged that Republican-led climate change hearings that had just concluded were a deep moral failure. Krugman described the GOP [Republican] US House of Representatives hearings at which of five invited witnesses on climate change, one was a lawyer, another an economist, and a third a professor of marketing—witnesses without any expertise in climate change science. One of the witnesses that was actually a scientist was expected to support the skeptical position but surprised everyone by supporting the mainstream scientific view on the amount of warming that the world has already experienced. Yet he was immediately attacked by climate skeptics.

The point of the Krugman article is that it is obvious from the witnesses who were asked to testify that the GOP-led hearings were never meant to be a serious attempt to understand climate change science. In this regard, Krugman says:

> But it's worth stepping back for a moment and thinking not just about the science here, but about the morality.
>
> For years now, large numbers of prominent scientists have been warning, with increasing urgency, that if we continue

with business as usual, the results will be very bad, perhaps catastrophic. They could be wrong. But if you're going to assert that they are in fact wrong, you have a moral responsibility to approach the topic with high seriousness and an open mind. After all, if the scientists are right, you'll be doing a great deal of damage.

But what we had, instead of high seriousness, was a farce: a supposedly crucial hearing stacked with people who had no business being there and instant ostracism for a climate skeptic who was actually willing to change his mind in the face of evidence. As I said, no surprise: as [politically active, early-twentieth-century author] Upton Sinclair pointed out long ago, it's difficult to get a man to understand something when his salary depends on his not understanding it.

But it's terrifying to realize that this kind of cynical careerism—for that's what it is—has probably ensured that we won't do anything about climate change until catastrophe is already upon us.

So on second thought, I was wrong when I said that the joke was on the GOP; actually, the joke is on the human race. [Paul Krugman, "The Truth, Still Inconvenient," *New York Times*, April 4, 2011.]

Sham Hearings Create an Ethical Problem

The central ethical problem with the US congressional hearings on climate change is entailed by the universally recognized duty of people and nations to prevent avoidable harm to others. . . . [All] major ethical theories recognize duties, obligations, and responsibilities of people to prevent serious harm to all people without regard to where they live around the world. . . .

Also . . . this duty to prevent harm is triggered once anyone is on notice that harms to others could be created by their actions, particularly when those harms could be grave. A corollary of this responsibility is that once someone is put on notice that their behavior could be creating great harm, one cannot avoid the duty to prevent harm to others by ignoring evidence that their behavior is causing harm. The behavior of the US Congress in the recent climate change hearings is deeply, ethically problematic because there was no serious attempt to understand the potential harms the United States was causing others through US emissions of greenhouse gases. In fact, the witnesses that were selected by Congress could not be seriously understood as a sincere effort to determine the nature of the threat entailed by climate change. One must assume the congressional hearings were designed to avoid what credible scientists or credible scientific institutions such as the [National] Academy of Sciences know about climate change.

This kind of behavior is often referred to in ethics as "willful ignorance." In the 13th century, [Dominican priest, theologian, and philosopher] Thomas Aquinas explained why "willful ignorance" is ethically problematic.

> It is clear that not every kind of ignorance is the cause of a sin, but that alone which removes the knowledge which would prevent the sinful act. . . . This may happen on the part of the ignorance itself, because, to wit, this ignorance is voluntary, either directly, as when a man wishes of set purpose to be ignorant of certain things that he may sin the more freely; or indirectly, as when a man, through stress of work or other occupations, neglects to acquire the knowledge which would restrain him from sin. For such like negligence renders the ignorance itself voluntary and sinful, provided it be about matters one is "bound and able to know." [Thomas Aquinas, *Summa*, 1265–1273.]

Without doubt, gathering information for the purpose of ignoring obligations that would flow from the relevant evidence is deeply, ethically troublesome. Because the impacts of climate change are so potentially devastatingly catastrophic to millions of poor people around the world, willful ignorance of

Anti-Environment Sentiment in Congress Is Widespread	
Votes targeted at the Environmental Protection Agency	50
Votes to undermine protection for public lands and coasts	33
Votes to block actions that prevent pollution	31
Votes to dismantle the Clean Air Act	28
Votes targeted at the Department of the Interior	25
Votes targeted at the Department of Energy	24
Votes to defund or repeal clean energy initiatives	22
Votes to block actions that address climate change	20
Votes to dismantle the Clean Water Act	16
Votes to dismantle the National Environmental Policy Act	11
Total anti-environment votes under GOP House majority in the 112th Congress	**125**

TAKEN FROM: "New Database Sheds Light on Anti-Environment Congress as Attacks on Public Protections Continue," Ombwatch.org, September 14, 2011.

climate change causation must be understood to be deeply, ethically reprehensible. This is particularly true because ... the duty to act on climate change is triggered long before all scientific uncertainties are resolved. ...

Reckless, Irresponsible Behavior Is Unethical

From the standpoint of ethics, those who engage in risky behavior are not exonerated because they did not know that their behavior would actually cause damage. Under law that implements this ethical norm, for instance, to be convicted of reckless driving or reckless endangerment, a prosecutor simply has to prove that the defendant acted in a way that he or she should have known to be risky. Many types of risky behavior are criminal because societies believe dangerous behavior is irresponsible and should not be condoned. As a matter of ethics, a relevant question in the face of scientific uncertainty about harmful consequences of human behavior is whether there is a reasonable basis for concluding that serious harm to others could result from the behavior. Yet, as we have seen, in the case of climate change, humans have understood the potential threat from climate change for over one hundred years and the scientific support for this concern has been building with increasing speed over the last 30 years. In fact, for more than 20 years, the IPCC [Intergovernmental Panel on Climate Change], a scientific body created with the strong support of governments around the world to advise them about the conclusions of peer-review climate change science, has been telling the world that the great harm from climate change is not only possible but likely with increasing levels of confidence. Moreover, since the late 1970s, the [National] Academy of Sciences has been advising the US government that human-induced climate change is a serious threat to human health and life and the natural systems on which life depends.

By the end of the 1980s, there was widespread understanding among climate change scientists around the world that there was a great threat posed by rising concentrations of atmospheric greenhouse gases even though there were considerable uncertainties about timing and magnitude of climate change impacts. The climate science that has been accumulating in the last 20 years has been increasing the confidence about timing and magnitude of climate change impacts according to the IPCC as well as reasons for concluding that recent warming is largely human caused notwithstanding considerable natural variability in the climate system. The United States Congress has clearly been on notice for several decades that climate change is a significant threat.

Congressional Hearings Are Ethically Bankrupt

Thus far we have seen that it's ethically unacceptable to willfully avoid evidence that would establish potential harm to others and that this duty stems from the clear ethical responsibility recognized by almost all ethical theories to prevent serious harm to others. We have also seen that even in the face of uncertainty about the harm, ethics requires action. Given what is at stake with climate change, the conduct of the recent US hearings on climate change is deeply, ethically bankrupt.

Krugman's condemnation of the recently concluded US congressional hearings on climate change is strongly supported by almost all ethical theories. Given what is at stake in climate change, the US Congress has a strong duty to examine the science of climate change carefully, using the most reliable scientific analyses and expertise. The United States created the [National] Academy of Sciences for the express goal of giving scientific advice to government. In a report in May 2010, the academy concluded that:

> A strong, credible body of scientific evidence shows that climate change is occurring, is caused largely by human activities, and poses significant risks for a broad range of human and natural systems. [National Academy of Sciences, "Advancing the Science of Climate Change," 2010.]

Given that the National Academy of Sciences was created for the express purpose of giving advice to the government about scientific issues and that Congress is now expressly ignoring the advice of the very institution created to summarize significant complex scientific issues, the recent hearings of Congress are even more ethically troubling than the moral failure in conducting the hearings.

> "The shortcomings of GINA [the Ge-
> netic Information Nondiscrimination
> Act] stem from the health finance sys-
> tem of the United States and the ab-
> sence of effective health privacy legisla-
> tion."

Biotechnology Legislation Raises Ethical Concerns About Privacy and Discrimination

Mark A. Rothstein

Mark A. Rothstein is the Herbert F. Boehl Chair of Law and Medicine and the director of the Institute for Bioethics, Health Policy and Law at the University of Louisville. In the following viewpoint, he expresses reservations about the potential effectiveness of a proposed federal law entitled the Genetic Information Nondiscrimination Act (GINA). Rothstein asserts that while the proposed legislation has noble intentions, its lack of specifics regarding patients' rights after diagnosis raises serious ethical questions about insurance coverage, employer involvement in private matters, and the medical treatment of genetically predicted illnesses. What is clearly needed to eliminate genetic discrimina-

Mark A. Rothstein, "Is GINA Worth the Wait?," *Journal of Law, Medicine, & Ethics,* Spring 2008, pp. 174–178. Copyright © 2008 by Mark Rothstein. All rights reserved. Reproduced by permission.

tion by insurance carriers, Rothstein declares, is for all individuals to have guaranteed health care coverage; to prevent employers from using or purchasing genetic information, Congress must remain vigilant.

As you read, consider the following questions:

1. According to Rothstein, why do many at-risk individuals decline genetic testing?

2. What does Rothstein suggest are four key problems that might result from the collection of genetic information for employment or health insurance records?

3. What does Rothstein consider the essential flaw of the proposed GINA legislation?

It has been pending in Congress for twelve years, despite the support of the last two presidential administrations and the National Institutes of Health. It has been the subject of extensive affirmative lobbying by academic medical centers, pharmaceutical and biotech companies, genetic disease advocacy groups, and civil rights organizations. It has overcome vehement objections by employers and insurers. Its final passage, however, has been thwarted by a few congressional leaders, who have prevented enactment despite overwhelming bipartisan support in both houses of Congress.

Based on this legislative history, one could not help but assume that the Genetic Information Nondiscrimination Act (GINA) is a revolutionary piece of legislation that, if finally enacted, would provide extensive, effective, and comprehensive protection against genetic discrimination in health insurance and employment. Unfortunately, such an assessment would be incorrect. Indeed, GINA may be a case of too much ado about too little. GINA is a fatally flawed bill, whose chances of achieving its noble goal of genetic nondiscrimination were doomed from the start by a health finance system in which individual health insurance is medically underwritten and by employment laws that fail to protect the privacy of employee health information.

This [viewpoint] puts GINA into perspective by reviewing the need for legislation, the bill's key provisions, and its likely consequences. The [viewpoint] also discusses the essential issues of discrimination and disclosure of genetic information in health insurance and employment that GINA does *not* address. It observes that the shortcomings of GINA stem from the health finance system of the United States and the absence of effective health privacy legislation. Upon closer inspection, discrimination based on "genetic information" is not a discrete and singular issue; it is a case study for the broader issue of the permissible uses and disclosures of predictive health information.

History of Genetic Nondiscrimination Laws

Health Insurance. Individual health insurance policies are medically underwritten on an individual basis. Health insurers consider the applicant's current health status and his or her likely future claims along with those of any dependents to be covered. Individual health insurance is regulated by the states. When the Human Genome Project [a scientific research project whose objective was to map the genetic makeup of the human species] officially began in 1990, the potential for genetic discrimination in health insurance was the first issue to receive the attention of scholars, policy analysts, and state legislatures. In 1993, the NIH/DOE [National Institutes of Health/Department of Energy] Task Force on Genetic Information and Insurance issued a report recommending that "[i]nformation about past, present, or future health status, including genetic information, should not be used to deny health care coverage or services to anyone." State legislatures, often responding to intense lobbying efforts by consumer advocates and researchers, soon began enacting bans on genetic discrimination in individual health insurance. By the end of 2007, the overwhelming majority of states had enacted laws prohibiting genetic discrimination in health insurance.

Group health policies are group underwritten. The claims experience of the group may affect renewability and rates, but individual risks are not considered and individuals are not treated differently in coverage or rates. Group health insurance is customarily issued through employer-sponsored group health plans, which may be either self-insured or commercially insured. Because group health plans are considered "employee welfare plans," they are subject to the federal Employee Retirement Income Security Act (ERISA). As to these plans, state laws prohibiting genetic discrimination in health insurance are preempted. In 1996, Congress enacted the Health Insurance Portability and Accountability Act (HIPAA), which amended ERISA in several respects. A little-discussed provision of HIPAA provides that neither group health plans nor health insurers offering group coverage may establish rules for eligibility of any individual or a dependent of the individual based on "genetic information." This means that genetic discrimination in employer-sponsored group health insurance, by far the largest source of health coverage, is illegal under federal law.

Employment. The first state laws prohibiting genetic discrimination in employment were enacted in Florida, Louisiana, and North Carolina in the early 1970s. These laws prohibited discrimination on the basis of the sickle-cell trait. In 1981, New Jersey prohibited discrimination in employment based on the following genetic traits: sickle cell, hemoglobin C, thalassemia, Tay-Sachs, or cystic fibrosis. These initial laws, prohibiting irrational discrimination against the unaffected carriers of recessive disorders, were followed by more comprehensive bans against discrimination on the basis of predictive genetic information. The laws typically prohibit employers from requiring or requesting a genetic test or using the results of a genetic test for a discriminatory purpose. The laws apply to all genetic disorders regardless of the mode of inheritance. By the end of 2007, approximately two-thirds of the states had enacted laws prohibiting genetic discrimination in employment.

At the federal level, Executive Order 13145 was issued in 2000. It prohibits genetic discrimination in federal employment based on genetic information. The order was intended to pave the way for legislation applicable to the private sector, but broader legal restrictions have not been enacted. The only other federal law relevant to genetic discrimination in employment is the Americans with Disabilities Act (ADA), which prohibits discrimination in employment on the basis of disability. In 1995, the Equal Employment Opportunity Commission issued a nonbinding interpretation that discrimination against individuals based on genetic predisposition was unlawful under the ADA. A subsequent series of Supreme Court cases, in which the court adopted a narrow view of the coverage of the ADA, convinced virtually all commentators that the ADA would *not* apply to asymptomatic individuals who were discriminated against on the basis of genetically increased risk of disease.

Need for GINA. Proposals for state and federal legislation prohibiting genetic discrimination in health insurance and employment began by the mid-1990s, preceding any evidence of significant discriminatory conduct by health insurers or employers. The demands for federal legislation have intensified over the years, despite enactment of numerous state genetic nondiscrimination laws and the continued absence of any significant evidence of discrimination. Why?

There is considerable evidence that numerous individuals who are genetically at risk for some serious disorders decline potentially efficacious genetic testing and medical intervention because they are concerned about the possibility of discrimination against themselves and family members. The supposed need for such defensive practices has motivated genetic disease advocacy and civil rights groups to support nondiscrimination legislation. In addition, genetics researchers, biotech companies, pharmaceutical companies, and genetic test developers realize that their efforts will be for naught unless individuals are willing to undergo genetic testing. Thus, researchers and commercial interests have been among the staunchest supporters of genetic nondiscrimination legislation. Federal legislation has been generally viewed as preferable to state legislation because it would be more consistent and comprehensive than the patchwork of state laws, even though GINA would not preempt more protective state laws.

There are four main concerns regarding the use of genetic information in employment and health insurance that have driven consumer efforts to obtain genetic nondiscrimination legislation. The same concerns also apply to the use of genetic information in life, disability, and long-term care insurance. First, individuals are concerned about having their health privacy invaded by commercial entities searching their health records for the existence of genetic information. Second, individuals fear they will be required to undergo genetic testing as a condition of health insurance or employment and thereby to confront information about their health risks that they would prefer not to know. Third, individuals worry that a health insurer or employer will misunderstand the significance of the genetic information, resulting in their being erroneously disqualified from a job or insurance.

Finally, individuals are concerned that even if the information is not misinterpreted, the results will be used to exclude them from access to something of great importance to them and to which they believe they have a degree of entitlement.

Health Insurance Provisions

GINA provides that a health insurer offering health insurance coverage in the individual market may not establish rules for eligibility or adjust premium or contribution amounts of any individual based on genetic information. Genetic information is defined as information about an individual's genetic tests, the genetic tests of family members, or the occurrence of a disease in family members of the individual. Genetic information does not include information about the sex or age of an individual.

Health insurers also may not request or require an individual or a family member of the individual to undergo a genetic test. The same restrictions also apply to insurers offering Medicare supplemental policies. GINA further provides that group health insurers, which are prohibited by HIPAA from discriminating in coverage and premiums based on genetic information, are required to comply with the privacy and confidentiality rules of HIPAA and are barred from requesting or requiring genetic information about a participant, family member, beneficiary, or enrollee prior to enrollment.

The health insurance provisions of GINA are similar to state laws prohibiting genetic discrimination in health insurance, but the approach of all of these laws is fundamentally flawed. Under GINA, it would be unlawful for an individual health insurer to discriminate against an individual because the individual's genetic test or family history puts the individual at increased risk of developing a disease or disorder. To take a common example, it would prohibit discrimination against a woman who tested positive for one of the genetic mutations associated with an increased risk of breast cancer. Nevertheless, after a period of time, assuming the woman developed breast cancer, GINA would provide no protection. GINA, like all of the state laws on the issue, would apply only to asymptomatic individuals. It would be a matter of state insurance law whether the insurer could decide not to renew the policy or to increase the rates substantially. Only a few states have guaranteed renewal laws.

This absence of protection for affected individuals is not a loophole or oversight. It is the essence of the problem, and its centrality is illustrated by any attempt to eliminate the problem. Thus, if Congress believed it to be unfair for a genetically predisposed woman who developed breast cancer to lose her health insurance, would it help for Congress to prohibit discrimination against women who are genetically predisposed to breast cancer as well as women who develop gene-influenced breast cancer? Such a law would protect the 5 to 10 percent of women who get breast cancer from known genetic causes, but it would not protect other women who get breast cancer from unknown causes. Would it help for Congress to enact legislation prohibiting discrimination against all women who are genetically predisposed to breast cancer or who develop breast cancer? What would be the moral basis for giving favorable treatment to women with breast cancer while permitting discrimination against all other women (and men) who have other types of cancer or other illnesses?

Genetic discrimination in health insurance is merely a symptom of the broader problem of the lack of distributive justice in an individual health insurance market based on individual medical underwriting. The problem cannot be solved by genetic nondiscrimination laws, but only by enacting laws requiring guaranteed issue, guaranteed renewal, community-rated individual health insurance, or some other form of health coverage that does not rely on individual underwriting. The issue will persist until Congress enacts legislation providing that sick people and those likely to get sick have a right to health care coverage.

Employment Provisions

GINA would make it an unlawful employment practice for an employer, employment agency, labor organization, or training program to refuse to hire or to discharge any applicant or employee, or otherwise to discriminate against any employee with respect to compensation, terms, conditions, or privileges of employment based on genetic information. The definition of genetic information is the same for employment as for health insurance, mentioned above.

GINA also would make it unlawful for an employer, employment agency, labor organization, or training program to request, require, or purchase genetic information about an employee. One key exception is that it would be permissible for an employer to undertake genetic monitoring of the biological effects of toxic substances in the workplace if: the employer provides written notice to the employee; the employee provides prior, knowing, voluntary, and written authorization, or the monitoring is required by law; the employee is informed of individual monitoring results; the monitoring is in compliance with any applicable federal or state laws; and the employer receives only aggregate information that does not identify individual employees.

Despite the seemingly comprehensive prohibition on employer acquisition of genetic information, it is likely that employers would continue to obtain genetic information on a routine basis. In accordance with section 102(d)(3) of the ADA, after a conditional offer of employment, employers are permitted to require, as a condition of employment, that individuals submit to a medical examination and sign an authorization for the release of their health records. There are no limits on the scope of the examination or the records disclosed, although conditional offers may be withdrawn for medical reasons only if the examination or records indicate that the individual, with or without reasonable accommodation, is unable to perform the essential functions of the job.

Each year in the United States, conditional offerees sign an estimated 10.2 million authorizations for release of their health records. Because of the increasing interoperability of electronic health record networks, health record disclosures are becoming more comprehensive. Even if GINA resulted in employers requesting that custodians of health records (e.g., health care providers) release only nongenetic health information, there is no practical way to do so, and the entities are likely to continue the practice of routinely sending all of an individual's records. Thus, the number one concern of individuals today, that employers have access to their genetic test results, would remain their number one concern even if GINA were enacted. Effective protection of genetic information in the employment setting requires a ban on employer requests for comprehensive records at the post-offer stage; the research, development, and adoption of health information technology to facilitate the disclosure of only job-related health information; and the legal requirement to limit the scope of disclosures to job-related information.

Genetic Exceptionalism

GINA, like numerous state genetic nondiscrimination laws, is based on an approach known as "genetic exceptionalism." This means that genetic information is treated separately and differently from other health information. To many observers and elected officials, the need for "genetic" nondiscrimination legislation has seemed self-evident to address what has been regarded as a "genetic" discrimination problem. For others, genetic exceptionalism represents poor public policy for the following reasons: (1) it is impossible to define "genetic" when scientists have identified that genes play a role in virtually every human health problem; (2) it is impossible to isolate genetic information in health records; (3) a general law is easier to apply than separate laws for various health conditions; (4) having a separate law for genetic information increases the stigma associated with genetic conditions; and (5) it is difficult to make a moral argument that it is impermissible to discriminate against people on the basis of genetic information but that it is permissible to do so if the condition is not genetic.

Although enacting a genetic-specific law, such as GINA, might be easier than enacting more sweeping reforms, there are drawbacks to following the most politically expedient path. Fears of genetic discrimination in individual health insurance cannot be resolved unless legislation is enacted giving individuals the right of access to health insurance or health care irrespective of their current or likely future health condition. Fears of genetic discrimination in employment cannot be allayed without enacting legislation limiting the ability of employers to access comprehensive health records of individuals applying for jobs. It is unclear whether GINA would be a catalyst to overcoming these larger problems or serve to delay the enactment of more meaningful reforms.

The main value of GINA is its symbolism. If enacted, federal law would declare a national policy against discrimination in health insurance and employment on the basis of genetic information. The symbolic value of many other forms of anti-discrimination laws has led to widespread changes in attitudes and actions by private parties. Enacting this legislation, however, is not without risks. First, the law's genetic exceptionalism approach could serve to increase the stigma of genetic conditions, genetic tests, and genetic information. Second, individuals might be convinced by public pronouncements of the value of GINA and rely upon it to their detriment, such as by undergoing predictive genetic testing and subsequently having their test results released to future employers. Third, perhaps the greatest risk posed by enacting GINA would be that lawmakers might become complacent and believe that the problem of genetic discrimination in health insurance and employment has been adequately addressed by the new federal law.

> "If ethics is, as many people agree, a matter of core values such as honesty, fairness, and responsibility, then Congress indeed has lapsed into moral decline."

The US Economic Recession Is Closely Linked to Unethical Behavior in Congress

Rushworth M. Kidder

Rushworth M. Kidder was the founder of the Institute for Global Ethics, a nonprofit organization that seeks to promote ethics as an important element of human interaction. In the following viewpoint, he maintains that Congress's maliciousness, partisanship, and failure to compromise can be attributed to an absence of ethical behavior on the part of its members. Kidder illustrates what he views as a general ethical recession by comparing Congress's overall performance with its dismal approval rating in several public opinion polls. Partisan bickering over the debt ceiling during the summer of 2011, he adds, furthered the perception that Congress's ethical recession is a leading factor in the US economic recession.

As you read, consider the following questions:

1. In Kidder's opinion, what role did unethical behavior play in the 2008 financial collapse and subsequent recession?

2. How does Kidder approach the measurement of the dimensions of an ethical recession?

3. Does Kidder believe that Congress will put aside incompetence and partisanship and start acting more ethical in the future?

A re we in a double-dip ethics recession?

There's lots of speculation these days about a recurrent economic recession. The latest *New York Times* [NYT]/CBS News poll . . . found that a majority of Americans feel the nation is either headed into, or already is in, a recession.

When the last recession began to hit in 2008, we at the institute [Institute for Global Ethics] started examining evidence of a connection between economics and ethics. As scandal after scandal erupted in the financial sector—with unethical behavior taking down empires as vast as Bernie Madoff and Countrywide Financial—we asked whether the economic collapse arose not from innocent financial forces but from a vast ethical meltdown. Summarizing our work in 2009, we published *The Ethics Recession: Reflections on the Moral Underpinnings of the Current Economic Crisis*.

So we were pleased to see the Financial Crisis Inquiry Commission explicitly making the ethics link in its 545-page report last February [in 2011]. Pointing to "a systemic breakdown in accountability and ethics" as one of six fundamental causes of the crisis, its authors noted that "the integrity of our financial markets and the public's trust in those markets are essential to the economic well-being of our nation." But while they singled out the collapse in integrity—listing it as one of their six key findings, in fact—the authors never developed their case.

Quantifying an Ethics Recession

And that got us wondering whether we could put a metric to the idea of an ethics recession. For economists, *recession* is a term of art: Broadly speaking, they happen when GDP [gross domestic product] has been shrinking for two consecutive quarters. By analogy, might an ethics recession happen when a nation's public integrity has been in decline for a similar period? And if so, how might you measure that?

One way is through public opinion. Last week [in September 2011], after President [Barack] Obama's economic address to Congress, the pollsters posed an old chestnut to the public. Do you feel, they asked, that "things in this country" are generally "going in the right direction," or have things "pretty seriously gotten off on the wrong track"?

The question, which has been asked by the *New York Times*/CBS News since January 1991, is deliberately broad. After all, "things in this country" could mean much more than just the economy. And since the question explicitly asks about the distinction between right and wrong—which is how most Americans define *ethics*—it might provide a useful moral barometer.

But like any barometer, the reading is meaningful only when you know whether it's rising or falling. When the latest poll finds that 23 percent of the public thinks things are going right, that doesn't tell you much, so bear with me while we do the numbers.

In the George W. Bush administration, as the United States came gloriously together following 9/11 [the September 11, 2001, terrorist attacks on the United States], nearly two-thirds of the nation said we were on the right track. By the end of

Ethics May Influence Economic Decisions Like Government Bailouts

Not all bailouts are alike. Some bailouts, such as bailouts of depository institutions insured by the federal government, are routine and usually proceed according to a prearranged script. Although government officials exercise some discretion, statutes and regulations define parameters of government decision making. Federal institutions such as the FDIC [Federal Deposit Insurance Corporation], staffed mostly by career officials, administer these bailouts. Ethics problems have an impact, but the impact is less because government officials have less discretion and decisions are less arbitrary.

Other bailouts are extraordinary because they involve companies that ordinarily would be allowed to fail. Policy makers sometimes decide that these companies are too big to fail or that for some other reason they should not fail. These government decisions are highly discretionary. There are no prearranged legal rules or institutions to implement rules. Political appointees make most of these decisions, and sometimes the decisions can appear arbitrary (e.g., Bear Stearns and AIG are bailed out, but Lehman Brothers is not). When conflicts of interest and other ethics problems contribute to arbitrariness in government decisions regarding extraordinary bailouts, officials may misspend public money, eroding public confidence in government. This unpredictability may also cause capital markets to react adversely.

Richard W. Painter,
"Bailouts: An Essay on Conflicts of
Interest and Ethics When Government Pays the Tab,"
McGeorge Law Review, *vol. 41, 2009.*

Bush's second term, that enthusiasm had evaporated: In October 2009, only 7 percent said things were right, a low point never seen before or since.

Five months into the Obama administration, however, in May 2009, we'd bounced back up to 45 percent. And then came the deluge—down to 29 percent last November [2010], up to 36 percent in February of 2011, and finally into steady decline through March (30 percent), June (29 percent), and September (23 percent). That's enough to qualify as an "official" ethics recession.

Congress Earns Record Disapproval

Even more telling is the public's view of how Congress does its job. From a post-9/11 rating of 67 percent, congressional approval slipped to 12 percent at the end of the Bush administration in October 2008, which at the time was the lowest rating since NYT/CBS pollsters first launched the question. By April 2009, in the honeymoon of the Obama administration, the new Congress had climbed back to 28 percent. And then, again, the decline—to 24 percent last February [2011] and 20 percent in June, before crumbling in September to 12 percent, tying the record for public disgust.

But enough numbers. What do they tell us? They point to a devastating lack of confidence in Congress and the administration—indeed, in everything we call *Washington*. In interviews with some of the respondents to their poll, the NYT/CBS team heard expressions of deep disappointment with the self-serving bickering and small-minded rants they saw in Congress during the debt-ceiling debate over the summer. They long for a Congress that works.

But are these issues of ethics, or simply of incompetence or partisanship? If ethics is, as many people agree, a matter of core values such as honesty, fairness, and responsibility, then Congress indeed has lapsed into moral decline. Its institutional behavior over the summer [of 2011] raised serious questions about the truthfulness of what both sides portrayed as facts, about the sense of justice and fairness to citizens present and future, and about the duty of elected officials to find ways to compromise in order to prevent stalemate and paralysis. The public, appalled by the spectacle, sent congressional approval crashing by 8 points in three months.

Ethics isn't economics, and this measure is only an analogy. But if congressional behavior over the summer is, as many believe, a chief reason why an economy that seemed to be improving suddenly began spluttering again, the underlying cause well may lie in the new ethics recession.

> "How big of a scandal does it take to make a congressional candidate unelectable? This year [2010], if you're a Republican, it has to be pretty darn big."

Poor Oversight and Prioritizing Politics over Ethics Lead to the Election of Corrupt Lawmakers

Nick Baumann

Nick Baumann reports on social and political issues for Mother Jones. *In the following viewpoint, he comments on the questionable ethical conduct of former US attorney Tom Marino, a Republican from Pennsylvania's Tenth Congressional District who was running for the US House of Representatives at the time. According to Baumann, Marino is accused of improperly using his position in the Department of Justice to help Louis De-Naples—a friend and convicted felon with reputed Mafia connections—obtain a gambling license from the Pennsylvania state gaming commission. Baumann offers evidence to illustrate the specific ethics violations of which Marino could be accused, and he concludes that ultimately, even if voters disapprove of Marino, they will still vote for him rather than for a Democratic Party candidate.*

As you read, consider the following questions:

1. How does Baumann characterize the Department of Justice's regulations about US attorneys offering references?

2. According to Baumann, why is Tom Marino's behavior considered unethical?

3. In Baumann's opinion, why does Tom Marino stand an excellent chance of winning his election, even though he is being investigated for ethics violations?

How big of a scandal does it take to make a congressional candidate unelectable? This year [2010], if you're a Republican, it has to be pretty darn big.

Take GOP [Republican] House candidate Tom Marino in Pennsylvania's Tenth [Congressional] District, located in the northeast corner of the state. As a US attorney, Marino gave a reference to his "close friend" Louis DeNaples, a convicted felon his office investigated for potential mob ties. When the Department of Justice [DOJ] reportedly launched an investigation into the reference, Marino resigned, and got a job working as DeNaples' in-house lawyer.

Since then, Marino has offered several different stories about whether he was authorized to give DeNaples the reference in the first place. (He wasn't.) But the scandal, which Marino's Dem opponent, Rep. Chris Carney, has harped upon in ads and speeches, seems to have had little impact on Marino's chances of ousting the two-term incumbent Blue Dog Dem. Nate Silver, the *New York Times*' polling guru, gives Marino a stunning 74 percent chance of winning on Tuesday [in November 2010].

A Favor Raises Ethical Concerns

DeNaples, who was convicted of defrauding the government of more than half a million dollars in the 1970s, needed a reference so he could obtain a license from the state gaming commission to operate slot machines at the Mount Airy Lodge, a resort he owns in eastern Pennsylvania. In 2005, Marino provided that reference.

According to reporting by the *Allentown Morning Call*'s Matt Birkbeck, Marino's assistants learned about the reference in 2006, after they had launched a perjury investigation into DeNaples' statements about his relationship to the Scranton-based Bufalino crime family. Marino's assistants reported the conflict of interest to the Justice Department, which recused Marino's entire office from the case and transferred it to another district. Then the DOJ launched an internal investigation into Marino's conduct. The probe was closed when Marino resigned in 2007 to work for DeNaples.

On at least two occasions—in an interview with a local newspaper reporter last September and a radio appearance this April—Marino claimed that he had provided the reference only after receiving permission from his superiors at the Justice Department. That wasn't true—at least according to the DOJ.

On September 28, Marino conceded that he never received permission to give the reference, and told the *Sunbury Daily Item* that he was allowed to give such references provided he "didn't use his job title or attempt to promote individuals on his staff." That meshes a bit with Justice Department guidelines, which say US attorneys shouldn't use their "position or title" to "coerce; to endorse any product, service or enterprise; or to give the appearance of governmental sanction."

Unfortunately for Marino, it is highly possible that he *did* in fact use his job title to provide the reference for DeNaples. The Pennsylvania state gaming commission has not released DeNaples' application for the slots license. But blank license

applications clearly indicate that references must include their occupations and business addresses. So if Marino filled out the form correctly, he also revealed his occupation when he provided the reference for DeNaples.

Marino's Recusal Implies He Had Knowledge of Committing an Ethics Violation

There's also little doubt that Marino's recusal from the De-Naples investigation constitutes an admission that there was a potential ethics issue involved in providing the reference. Justice Department rules mandate recusal "only where a conflict of interest exists or there is an appearance of a conflict of interest or loss of impartiality." Deborah Rhode, a legal ethics expert at Stanford Law School, says "it suggests that there is a relationship there that may be compromised by a conflict of interest," cautioning that some of the details of the case remain confidential and she is only familiar with what has been reported publicly.

It's clear that Marino feels the DeNaples story is damaging to his campaign. In mid-October, he told the *Scranton Times-*

Tribune he didn't want to take any more questions on the controversy. His spokesman did not return a call requesting comment. (Carney's office also did not respond to interview requests.) Not taking questions "looks bad on multiple levels," says Rhode. "This kind of conduct by a candidate is deeply problematic."

I also asked Kent Kauffman, a legal and business ethics expert at Indiana University-Purdue University Fort Wayne, to analyze the situation. Here's part of what he wrote:

> If the allegations made against Mr. Marino are accurate, at least three, and perhaps up to five, federal regulations on Department of Justice employee ethics are at issue. 5 CFR 2635.702(b) (on Misuse of Position) allows a DOJ employee to "sign a letter of recommendation using his official title only in response to a request for an employment recommendation or character reference based upon personal knowledge of the character of an individual with whom he has dealt in the course of Federal employment or whom he is recommending for Federal employment."

> If the gaming license reference doesn't qualify as a 'letter of recommendation' under the Code of Federal Regulations, then this rule might not apply. However, if the reference document required the listing of the referent's business position, then a question could be raised that Mr. Marino used his official title, which would seem to show that the reference was based on the underlying DOJ investigation. That rule's focus is on the recommender's knowledge of the recommended party coming from DOJ employment.

> If Mr. Marino were to claim that the reference he gave to Mr. DeNaples was purely personal in nature and not official, that would seem to fly in the face of the purpose of a reference made to support someone's business activities. When seeking such a reference, it would seem to be implicit that the title of the reference provider is more important than his or her name and address.

Kauffman also cited other Justice Department rules on misuse of position, impartiality, and personal relationships as potentially problematic for Marino.

Ideology Trumps Ethics in Elections

Even right-wing activists have had their doubts about Marino. In March, during the primary, Zach Oldham, a RedState.com contributor, wrote a post calling Marino the "GOP's Giannoulias"—a reference to Illinois Senate candidate Alexi Giannoulias, whom Republicans have accused of being a "mob banker." (RedState chief Erick Erickson promoted the post to the site's front page.) Here's how Oldham wrapped up:

> One of the keys to a Republican resurgence is not only en-suring we have credibly conservative candidates running for office, but also candidates with a personal and professional record we can be proud of and defend. Tom Marino doesn't fit the bill.

I recently asked Oldham if he still feels the same way about Marino. He responded via Twitter:

> ... to be honest, I haven't paid attn to that race post-primary, but I'm sure he's better than Carney.

According to the polls, a lot of the voters in the district feel the same way. Marino may have a pretty big scandal to deal with. But at least he's not a Democrat.

> *"If compromise is a political and constitutional necessity, and if mutual respect is a moral requirement of our founding principles, then developing politics of civility is essential."*

Ethics and Morality in Congress Are Essential to Sustain Constitutional Rights and a Functional Democracy

David E. Skaggs

David E. Skaggs is a Colorado Democrat who served in the US House of Representatives from 1987 to 1999. Currently, he is the co-chairman of the Office of Congressional Ethics. In the following viewpoint, Skaggs argues that the US Constitution establishes a set of core principles for ethical bipartisan conduct in Congress. He also maintains that there are a number of practical steps members of Congress can take to foster civility toward one another, including allowing committees more time to work together, allowing full debate on more bills, and participating in bipartisan retreats. Without a spirit of compromise grounded in a commitment to honor the moral and ethical principles in the Constitution, Skaggs concludes, the hard work of solving America's problems cannot take place.

As you read, consider the following questions:

1. In Skaggs's opinion, why is the exercise of congressional power, as defined by the Constitution, so cumbersome?

2. Why are elected representatives obliged to treat each other with civility, according to Skaggs?

3. In Skaggs's judgment, what new initiatives implemented by House Speaker John Boehner will likely create a more collegial atmosphere in the US House of Representatives?

The challenges of managing a divided government became clear after last fall's [2010's] midterm election and soon will be clearer still. Concern about the nastiness of our politics multiplied after the awful attack on Congresswoman Gabrielle Giffords [who survived an assassination attempt by a deranged assailant on January 8, 2011], and many politicians pledged to do something about it.

While there's been more talk of bipartisan cooperation in Washington lately, and even two short-term budget agreements, showdowns loom over the debt ceiling and a budget deal for the remainder of the federal fiscal year.

Much of the talk suggests that bipartisanship is just a matter of making nice—more a matter of style than substance. If members of Congress see it that way, it won't have much staying power. In fact, bipartisanship and the civility it requires are a political, and even moral, necessity. Let me explain.

The argument flows from the philosophical foundation of the republic and its constitutional architecture.

Equality Demands Mutual Respect

Thomas Jefferson stated the core principles in the Declaration of Independence: We are all created equal, endowed with certain unalienable rights. Government exists to protect those rights, and the legitimacy of government—its "just powers"—depends on the consent of the governed.

The Constitution elaborates on these principles, starting with its aspirational preamble. It requires the consent of the governed be exercised through representative institutions, the essence of a republic. It then constrains those institutions with a system of checks and balances.

Even as it sets out other powers and responsibilities needed for effective national government, the Constitution makes the exercise of power cumbersome, in order to ensure that it is deliberative. This constitutional scheme itself tends to drive policy to the center. We do not have a parliamentary system in which a party wins a majority of seats and is entitled to govern. In our system, the necessity for compromise springs from our constitutional DNA.

Now, consider the political profile of the country. As the last two elections confirmed, we are a politically centrist people, split pretty much down the middle. The country's political makeup should also counsel bipartisan cooperation.

It's one thing to make a constitutional and political case for bipartisanship and civility. It's quite another to encourage and sustain it. Like all of us, members of Congress respond to ideas and to incentives. The good news is that our founding principles furnish the ideas, and political realities should help with the incentives.

America's leading idea was and is that we're all created equal. To keep faith with that principle, our representatives need to act out of the mutual respect that equality demands. As elected representatives of constituencies of civic equals, they are obliged to treat one another civilly.

Out of this flows an imperative for civility as a matter of political morality. That is, if compromise is a political and constitutional necessity, and if mutual respect is a moral requirement of our founding principles, then developing politics of civility is essential. This civility stuff is worthy enough in its own right. It makes the business of politics more pleasant. However, it is also the means needed to reach the goal of bipartisan compromise.

The Human Dimension of Bipartisanship

That gets us to a human dimension, where psychology, sociology, and politics mix.

We're most likely to feel able to compromise with people we trust. We're only likely to trust those we've gotten to know. People are not likely to get well acquainted with colleagues who do not treat them decently. We usually look for some minimal show of goodwill from others—especially if they are from another tribe (party).

It follows that civil and respectful behavior among our representatives is essential for them to develop the trust that in turn enables the bipartisan compromises that are needed for contemporary American politics to function.

Being nicer to one another won't get the job done by itself. Democratic and Republican representatives of goodwill must still do the heavy lifting of working out the compromises needed to solve our problems. But if they choose not to behave well toward one another, progress will almost certainly remain elusive. (And sometimes you wonder whether a certain level of hostility isn't a convenient excuse for avoiding the hard work of compromise.)

Practical and Fruitful Steps Toward Bipartisan Compromise

If you spend any time talking with members of Congress about their workplace and job satisfaction, you quickly learn

Bipartisan Cooperation Embodies Core American Values

In this hyper-partisan age, our representatives and senators need to know that we value partnership and cooperation—because both can make a positive impact here in the United States and around the world, particularly for those suffering from poverty and injustice.

It's up to us to tell Congress to work together to reflect America's best qualities: equality, generosity, and compassion.

Shawna Templeton, "A Cooperative Congress Can Save Lives," World Vision Blog, *May 4, 2012. http://blog.worldvision.org.*

that they don't enjoy being in the state of affairs at the Capitol any more than we enjoy watching it. So, can we anticipate some change in behavior?

In Congess's internally conflicted environment, an infusion of collegiality will help. So, give [House] Speaker John Boehner credit. By lengthening the House workweek, members will have more time in D.C. to do their work on a less frenzied schedule and more time to get acquainted with colleagues "across the aisle."

His plan to give more responsibility to House committees and to make more bills open to amendment and full debate in the House may also help. While arcane, these procedural changes give representatives a greater opportunity to spend time together working things out and being exposed to one another's points of view. That may help improve personal relationships.

There has even been mention of reviving the bipartisan retreats the House carried out from 1997 to 2003 in an effort to improve collegial relations and civility. The retreats included congressional families (a moderating influence now largely absent from Washington) and enabled these people simply to get to know one another in a friendly setting. It was nice to see what can happen when political adversaries meet holding their 4-year-olds in their arms—and appreciate what they have in common as parents.

In the end, it all depends on how these men and women choose to view their responsibility to the country and to one another. Let's hope they see the moral and practical imperative for bipartisan cooperation.

"After suffering crushing losses ... Republicans are not in a mood to tolerate another nasty scandal. The common expression among leaders is that they must 'clean house.'"

Punishment for Ethical Violations Is Swift and Decisive When Political Interests Are Threatened

Fred Barnes

Fred Barnes is the executive editor of the Weekly Standard. *In the following viewpoint, he comments on the steps Republican leaders in the House of Representatives have begun to take to purge corrupt GOP lawmakers from office. In Barnes's judgment, the Republican leadership of the House has grave concerns about the public reaction to the sex and corruption scandals that have plagued the party in recent years. To minimize their party's loss of congressional seats in the 2008 elections, Barnes observes, these leaders are acting swiftly to force any House Republicans implicated in a scandal to retire from office. Such rapid and decisive punishment, Barnes concludes, is unprecedented and reflects a lack of tolerance for moral and ethical lapses when political interests are at risk.*

As you read, consider the following questions:

1. Why does Barnes believe that the Larry Craig sex scandal will be so damaging to the impending congressional election campaign for Republicans?

2. According to Barnes, what effective tactic does the GOP leadership of the House of Representatives use to force corrupt Republican lawmakers to retire?

3. In Barnes's judgment, do Republicans in the Senate act more or less swiftly than their counterparts in the House to remove corrupt members from office?

Republicans are so intent on pushing scandal-plagued members of Congress out of office and far from the media spotlight that the entire party—from the White House to congressional leaders to the Republican National Committee to various campaign committees—was instantly united last week [in September 2007] in the effort to force Senator Larry Craig of Idaho to resign.

At another time, Republicans might have cut Craig some slack, allowing him to finish his term and not seek reelection. But after suffering crushing losses in last year's [2006's] midterm election—spurred in part by highly publicized GOP corruption in Congress—Republicans are not in a mood to tolerate another nasty scandal. The common expression among leaders is that they must "clean house."

They were already doing so when the story broke last week of Craig's arrest and subsequent guilty plea for disorderly conduct in an airport men's room notorious as a spot for anonymous gay sex. House Republicans had quietly coaxed Rep. Rick Renzi of Arizona into announcing his retirement next year. And with at least one more forced retirement expected, the corruption issue was being taken care of, belatedly but decisively.

A Sordid Sex Scandal

But the Craig case suddenly overshadowed the house-cleaning drive. His arrest had "global implications," a [George W.] Bush administration official says, because everyone has heard of it and knows the sordid details. Within hours of the disclosure of his arrest, Republicans decided Craig must go. Rarely have Republican leaders acted so swiftly as they did in sending the matter to the Senate Ethics Committee [the Senate Select Committee on Ethics] and stripping Craig of his seniority and ranking position on committees.

That was accompanied by calls for his resignation by John McCain and Norm Coleman and the promise that more of their Senate colleagues would follow suit in drumbeat fashion. In an unprecedented move, the national committee was prepared to urge Craig's immediate ouster. The message was clear.

The White House got involved, too. Presidential aides checked with leaders of the Bush reelection campaign in Idaho in 2004 and with Republican officials. They found no support for Craig, only a strong feeling that he should resign his seat immediately. For Craig, the string had run out, in Idaho as well as in Washington. Republicans are confident they can hold the Idaho seat in 2008.

What made the Craig case all the worse was its echo of the Mark Foley scandal that sideswiped Republicans a month before the 2006 election. After the Florida congressman's lewd e-mails with teenage Capitol pages were revealed, Republican House candidates across the country saw their poll numbers drop as much as 10 points. That all but assured Republicans would lose control of the House.

Zero Tolerance on Corruption

Republicans are desperate not to have another corruption-driven defeat in 2008. So when House Republican leader John Boehner, whip Roy Blunt, and others in the hierarchy met in a private retreat outside Washington last December, the corruption issue headed their agenda. They adopted a zero-tolerance policy. They want no House candidates with corruption problems on the ballot. In 2006, four House members resigned (two later went to jail).

Boehner came up with a vague phrase for the sort of scandal they had in mind. It's one with "a clear indication of serious transgressions." In Boehner's mind, an FBI [Federal Bureau of Investigation] raid on your home or your wife's office is such an indication.

Arizona's Renzi is under investigation by the U.S. attorney for land-swap legislation that might, if passed, have aided a political ally. After the office of his wife's insurance business was raided by the FBI, he gave up his post on the House Permanent Select Committee on Intelligence. That wasn't enough. Under pressure from Republican leaders, he announced his retirement in 2008.

An FBI raid on the Virginia home of Rep. John Doolittle of California has put him on the pariah list. He and his wife have ties to disgraced lobbyist Jack Abramoff, among other problems. Former supporters and financial backers have begun announcing (with the tacit approval of Republican leaders) their desire for him to retire.

If all else fails, the ultimate tool to force a retirement or resignation is to inform the House member or senator that the national party will provide no campaign funds and perhaps even will finance a primary opponent. This tactic was used against Craig, along with the threat that Senate Republican leaders would, publicly and noisily, demand he resign.

In the House, Republicans have an informal watch list of members who've been reported to be under investigation but haven't been raided. These include Gary Miller of California and Don Young of Alaska, both in trouble over earmarks that aided backers or business associates.

US Senate Responds More Slowly to Corruption

Boehner has vowed to "act swiftly and decisively" to push corruption-tainted Republicans out of office. Things are less clear in the clubby atmosphere of the Senate. While Republicans quickly moved against Craig, they have held back from taking action against Senator Ted Stevens of Alaska.

Stevens is renowned for splurging on earmarks. And it's because of them that his home was raided by a joint IRS [Internal Revenue Service] and FBI team on July 30. Many friends and ex-aides appear to have benefited from his earmarks, either directly or indirectly. But unlike Craig, Stevens hasn't been charged with any wrongdoing or pleaded guilty. Republican officials say this explains the hands-off approach.

Stevens is running for his eighth term next year, and he's a strong favorite to win. But he's no longer unassailable in Alaska. A poll last month found his positive rating had dipped to 44 percent. And in a hypothetical Senate primary, he trailed popular governor Sarah Palin by 23 points.

In Idaho, Craig's last cry for help was a request to Governor "Butch" Otter and the other Idaho senator, Mike Crapo, to speak out about how much he'd done for the state over the years. They declined. And Craig was toast.

Periodical and Internet Sources Bibliography

The following articles have been selected to supplement the diverse views presented in this chapter.

Donald A. Brown	"The Worst Ethical Scandal in the US Congress: Climate Change?," ThinkProgress.org, August 12, 2010.
Stephanie Condon	"Ethics Questions Plague Congress as Financial Reform Heads to Obama," CBSNews.com, July 15, 2010.
Paul Driessen	"Global Warming Pork and Profits," *Washington Times*, February 19, 2007.
Tom Heneghan	"Ethics Angle Missing in Financial Crisis Debate," Reuters.com, March 4, 2010.
Amy L. McGuire and Mary Anderlik Majumder	"Two Cheers for GINA?," *Genome Medicine*, vol. 1, no. 1, 2009.
Jonathan D. Moreno and Michael Rugnetta	"New Stem Cell Policy Founded on Ethics and Expertise," Center for American Progress, March 18, 2009. www.americanprogress.org.
Brody Mullins and T.W. Farnam	"Lawmakers' Global-Warming Trip Hit Tourist Hot Spots," *Wall Street Journal*, August 8, 2009.
Adam Serwer	"The GOP Plan to Give Your Boss 'Moral' Control over Your Health Insurance," *Mother Jones*, February 14, 2012.
George Skaggs	"The Elusive Lessons of Ethics and Accountability," TheGraph.com, December 6, 2010.
Peter J. Wallison	"The True Story of the Financial Crisis," *American Spectator*, May 2011.

OPPOSING VIEWPOINTS® SERIES

CHAPTER 3

How Do Lobbying and Ethics Reform Measures Affect Congressional Ethics?

Chapter Preface

Earmarks are funding requests for special projects that legislators in Congress add to large appropriations bills such as the annual budget of the federal government. Although earmark funding is relatively small when compared to the enormous amount of money allocated to the overall spending bill, such requests can account for tens to hundreds of millions of taxpayer dollars. Fiscal hawks, concerned taxpayers, and reform advocates typically view earmarks as an unethical misappropriation of federal funds without proper institutional oversight that only serves to benefit an individual legislator, his or her constituents, or a special interest group that has lobbied the legislator. On the contrary, supporters of earmarks maintain that the Constitution endows Congress with the power to direct funding as it sees fit. These proponents also assert that if Congress does not perform its duty, the executive branch could overstep its constitutional authority and make funding decisions without the consent of the legislative branch. Finally, advocates of earmarking point out that the practice accounts for only a tiny percentage of federal spending as a whole— earmarks accounted for less than .05 percent of federal spending in fiscal year 2010 before Congress voluntarily put an end to the practice of adding earmarks to appropriations bills.

Prior to Congress's decision to place a moratorium on earmark spending, the practice raised a number of ethical questions regarding a legislator's motivation for inserting such funding requests into an appropriations bill. A principal concern involves a legislator's ability to use the large pool of federal funding to benefit a limited number of constituents in his or her own district. A classic example of this practice occurred in 2005 when Senator Ted Stevens (a Republican from Alaska) attempted to earmark $223 million in federal funding to build a bridge between a small Alaskan town with a population of fewer than nine thousand people and an island with a population of fifty. The public outcry resulting from this news report led to the removal of funding for the so-called "Bridge to Nowhere" from the federal spending bill. Other ethical considerations concern the receipt of direct or indirect benefits awarded to the legislator, his or her family members, or close friends. Prior to lobbying reform measures implemented in the 2000s, lobbyists often wooed members of Congress with private jet access, luxury vacations, campaign donations, and other perks in exchange for their tacit agreement to attach earmark requests to spending bills that would benefit the corporations that the lobbying firms represented. There are also ethical implications for legislators who use earmarks as bargaining chips to gain support for a special funding project or a specific ideological agenda. In a blog for Breitbart.com, Drew Johnson condemns this practice, asserting that "earmarks are nothing more than bribes to buy the votes of members of Congress who don't have the brains to think for themselves or the backbones to stand up for their beliefs."

Yielding to widespread public outrage in response to its perceived abuse of earmark spending, Congress imposed a voluntary moratorium on earmarks in 2010. However, as Johnson observes, "the moratorium has more loopholes than a doughnut shop." The loss of transparency in funding requests undermines earmark reforms implemented in the mid-2000s that required a legislator to identify himself or herself publicly with a proposed earmark, to make draft copies of bills or amendments that contained the requested earmark available to the public, and to certify that his or her family and friends would receive no benefit from the earmark. Recently, some legislators have called upon Congress to lift the earmark moratorium in an effort to loosen partisan gridlock surrounding stalled legislation. However, other legislators view such bargaining tactics as an ineffective means by which to achieve political consensus. Instead, they argue that the temporary moratorium should be made into a permanent ban on earmarks. Such a political position is welcome news to government watchdog groups such as Citizens Against Government Waste (CAGW), which states, "Until a ban is established, taxpayers will be justified in their belief that members of Congress are being creative and deceptive in skirting the moratorium and continuing to obtain earmarks."

The moratorium on earmarks is one example of an attempt to ensure the integrity of Congress's allocation of taxpayers' dollars. The viewpoints in this chapter also examine the legislation passed in an effort to address the ethical and legal challenges presented by lobbying and a lack of transparency in government.

| "We can begin to restore faith in this institution by divesting ourselves of some of the perks and privileges that have somehow crept into public service."

Lobbying and Ethics Reform Legislation Is Crucial to Restore Congressional Integrity

John McCain

John McCain is a five-term senator from Arizona. He was also the Republican nominee for president in 2008. In the following viewpoint, McCain urges the passage of a law that would reform ethical standards in the Senate by drastically limiting the influence of lobbyists on members of that body. The bill calls for the elimination of free meals and sports and entertainment tickets; the cessation of travel on corporate jets at first-class ticket rates; increased regulation of earmark funding in appropriations bills; and the creation of an office of public integrity to investigate corruption in the Senate. McCain strongly advocates for the bill's passage, concluding that the reforms it entails would go a long way toward restoring the public's trust in its elected representatives. The bill was introduced in Congress on January 7, 2007, but it was never enacted.

John McCain, "Senator McCain Statement on Lobbying and Ethics Reform Bill," McCain.senate.gov, January 4, 2007.

As you read, consider the following questions:

1. What does McCain mean by the "revolving door" perk available to Congress members?

2. How does McCain want to reform the current rule regarding congressional travel on corporate jets?

3. According to McCain, by how many percentage points did the use of earmarks increase between 1994 and 2005?

Mr. President, today I am pleased to be joined by Senators [Russ] Feingold, [Susan] Collins, and [Joseph] Lieberman in introducing a bill to provide greater transparency into the process of influencing our government and to ensure greater accountability among public officials.

The legislation proposes a number of important and necessary reforms. It would provide for faster reporting and greater public access to reports filed by lobbyists and their employers under current law. It would require greater disclosure of lobbyists' contributions and payments to lawmakers and entities associated with them, as well as fund-raising and other events they host. The bill also would require greater disclosure from both lobbyists, and members and employees of Congress, of travel that is arranged or financed by a lobbyist or his client.

Curbing the Influence of Lobbyists Is Crucial

To address the problem of the revolving door between government and the private sector, the bill would strengthen the lobbying restrictions on former senior members of the executive branch, former members of Congress, and former senior congressional staff. It would require that members publicly disclose negotiations they are having with prospective private employers to ensure there is no conflict of interest. The bill also would modify the provision in current law that exempts former federal employees who go to work for Indian tribes as outside lobbyists and agents from the revolving door laws.

The bill would prohibit all gifts from lobbyists to lawmakers and their staff. To ensure that such a ban is not circumvented, the bill also would require members of Congress and their staff to pay the fair market value for travel on private planes and the fair market value of sports and entertainment tickets. Members and staff would also have to post the details of their privately sponsored work trips online for public inspection.

The bill would establish an independent, nonpartisan Office of Public Integrity. Armed with a number of investigative tools, the Office of Public Integrity would investigate alleged misconduct by members and their staff and make appropriate recommendations to the Senate Ethics Committee [the Senate Select Committee on Ethics] for final disposition.

Finally, the bill would help us combat wasteful, pork-barrel spending. It would amend congressional rules to allow lawmakers to challenge unauthorized appropriations, earmarks, and policy riders in appropriations bills.

Mr. President, when I introduced similar legislation over a year ago, I regretted that such reform was even necessary. And, I voted against the bill that was ultimately passed in the Senate because it lacked a number of elements essential to true reform.

The American People Are Fed Up with Corruption

Unfortunately, the need for such reform has only become more acute. The American people's faith and confidence in this venerable institution has steadily eroded. The day after the midterm elections, CNN reported that, according to national exit polls, voters were concerned about corruption and

Lobbying Activity, 1998–2011

Year	Total Lobbying Spending	Number of Lobbyists
1998	$1.44 Billion	10,408
1999	$1.44 Billion	12,936
2000	$1.56 Billion	12,535
2001	$1.64 Billion	11,838
2002	$1.82 Billion	12,125
2003	$2.04 Billion	12,920
2004	$2.18 Billion	13,167
2005	$2.42 Billion	14,065
2006	$2.62 Billion	14,513
2007	$2.85 Billion	14,840
2008	$3.30 Billion	14,154
2009	$3.50 Billion	13,672
2010	$3.51 Billion	12,928
2011	$3.32 Billion	12,654

TAKEN FROM: Center for Responsive Politics, April 30, 2012.

ethics in government more than any other issue. I can tell you the polls, if not spot on, are not far off.

During my travels around the country last year [in 2006], it quickly became clear that there is a deep perception that we legislators do not act on the priorities of the American people, that special interests, and not the people's interests, guide our legislative hand. This loss in confidence is not limited to a single party or ideology; rather, it cuts across the spectrum. It is a perception bred by recent congressional failures and scandals, which I need not chronicle here. We can begin to restore faith in this institution by divesting ourselves of some of the perks and privileges that have somehow crept into public service.

Take for example, free meals and sports and entertainment tickets. The American people have rightfully come to see the abuse of such perks as a corrupting influence. In a string of guilty pleas last year, several lobbyists, former congressional aides, and a congressman admitted that such gifts were used as bribes. Quite frankly, there is no good reason why members of Congress and their staff cannot forgo such gifts from lobbyists. No one would seriously contend that they are necessary for us to conduct the people's business. A total gift ban would go a long way towards restoring the public's confidence in us.

Another critical aspect requiring reform is the ability of a member to travel on a corporate jet and only pay the rate of a first-class plane ticket. This bill requires senators and their employees who use corporate or charter aircraft to pay the fair market value for that travel. While I appreciate that such a change is not popular with some of my colleagues, the time has come to fundamentally change the way we do things in this town. Much of the public views our ability to travel on corporate jets, often accompanied by lobbyists, while only reimbursing the first-class rate, as a huge loophole in the current gift rules. And they are right—it is. I have no doubt that the average American would love to fly around the country on very comfortable corporate-owned aircraft and only be charged the cost of a first-class ticket. It is a pretty good deal we have got going here. We need to face the fact that the time has come to end this congressional perk.

A Nonpartisan Office of Public Integrity Is Needed

At a time when the public is questioning our integrity, the Senate needs to more aggressively enforce its own rules. We can do this not just by making more public the work that the Senate Ethics Committee currently undertakes, but by addressing the conflict that is inherent in any body that regulates itself. That is why I am again proposing the creation of a new Office of Public Integrity with the capacity to initiate and conduct investigations, uncolored by partisan concerns and unconstrained by collegial relationships.

Finally, Mr. President, if we are truly serious about reform, we need to address what some have coined the currency of corruption—earmarks. In 1994, there were 4,126 earmarks. In 2005, there were 15,877—an increase of nearly 400 percent! But there was a little good news for 2006 solely due to the good sense that occurred unexpectedly when the Labor HHS [Health and Human Services, Education and Related Services] appropriations bill was approved with almost no earmarks, an amazing feat given that there were over 3,000 earmarks the prior year for just that bill. Yet despite this first reduction in 12 years, it does not change the fact that the largest number of earmarks have still occurred in the last three years—2004, 2005, and 2006.

Now, let us consider the level of funding associated with those earmarks. The amount of earmarked funding increased from $23.2 billion in 1994 to $64 billion in FY [fiscal year] 2006. Remarkably, it rose by 34 percent from 2005 to 2006, even though the number of earmarks decreased! Earmarked dollars have doubled just since 2000, and more than tripled in the last 10 years. This explosion in earmarks led one lobbyist to deride the appropriations committees as favor factories. The time for us to fix this broken process is long overdue.

Mr. President, this past election, the American people sent a clear message: Clean up the way business is done in our capital. As faithful public servants, we are obligated to respond. Let us respond meaningfully, to assure the American people that we are here promoting the interests of Main Street over that of K Street [a major thoroughfare in Washington, DC], and that we are more interested in public service than the perks and privileges offered us. Let us also remind ourselves that we came here in the sincere belief that public service is a noble calling, a reward unto itself.

I therefore urge my colleagues in joining me on this bill. I think our nation and this venerable institution will be all the better for it.

> *"There is only one cure for this disease: a lifetime ban on members and staff lobbying Congress or associating in any way with for-profit lobbying efforts."*

Lobbying and Ethics Reform Legislation Does Not Address the Root Cause of Unethical Activity

Jack Abramoff

Jack Abramoff is a former congressional lobbyist who served four years in federal prison for his role in a lobbying scandal that involved defrauding Indian casinos. In the following viewpoint, he maintains that members of Congress and their staffers are eager to ingratiate themselves to lobbyists because their assistance could lead to a lucrative position of their own with a lobbying firm in the future. In Abramoff's judgment, the only way to eliminate unethical behavior between Congress and lobbyists is to ban elected officials and their aides from ever being able to accept a job with a lobbying firm.

As you read, consider the following questions:

1. What two crucial assets do former Congress members and their staffs have that make them attractive to lobbying firms, according to Abramoff?

2. What does Abramoff state is the most important reason that Congress members and their aides want to work with lobbyists?

3. How does Abramoff characterize existing rules regarding a "cooling off period" between leaving a job in Congress and accepting a job for a lobbying firm?

As I built what became the nation's largest individual lobbying practice—with 40 employees at its peak—I remained the only lobbyist in the firm who had not previously worked on Capitol Hill. Former Congress members and staff are everywhere on K Street, the lair of the lobbying world. Why? Because they have access.

That access was crucial to our lobbying efforts. If we couldn't get in the door, we couldn't present our client's case to decision makers. Hill veterans also had expertise. They knew the Byzantine legislative process and how to make it work for clients. Access and expertise: That's how the great lobbying machines work.

But that's not all.

I had many arrows in my lobbyist quiver to endear our firm to Congress: two fancy Washington restaurants that became virtual cafeterias for congressional staff, the best seats to every sporting event and concert in town, private planes at the ready to whisk members and staff to exotic locations, millions of dollars in campaign contributions ready for distribution. We had it all. But even with these corrupting gifts, nothing beat the revolving door.

During my time lobbying, I found that the vast majority of congressional staff I encountered wanted to get a job on K

Street. And why not? Their jobs on the Hill were only as secure as their boss's re-election prospects. Even then, they were never certain when they would encounter an office purge. The other side of the rainbow—K Street—was heavenly. Salaries were much higher. Perks were abundant. And lobbying is a growth industry, no matter which party is in office. As young staff members got married and had children, making the jump to K Street was often on their minds.

As I cultivated relationships on the Hill, or as the firm's lobbyists transformed their congressional friends into champions for our clients, I noticed the staff members craved a job on K Street far more than a fancy meal or a Washington Redskins ticket.

Most staff were fiercely loyal to their boss and to the institution they served. But, once they thought there was a chance to join our firm sometime down the line, they switched teams—psychologically first, and then in conduct. Understanding this, we would drop hints about the gilded life that awaited them on K Street, or share jokes with them about our future together as colleagues.

Staff members who thought they might be hired by our firm inevitably began acting as if they were already working for us. They seized the initiative to do our bidding. Sometimes, they even exceeded the lobbyists' wishes in an effort to win plaudits. From that moment, they were no longer working for their particular member of Congress. They were working for us. They would alert us to any inside information we needed to serve our clients. They would quash efforts to harm our clients, instead seeding appropriations and other benefits for them. I emphasize: They were working for us.

Our situation was not unique.

During my years as a lobbyist, I saw scores of congressional staff members become the willing vassals of K Street firms before soon decamping for K Street employment themselves. It was a dirty little secret. And it is a source of major corruption in Congress.

There is only one cure for this disease: a lifetime ban on members and staff lobbying Congress or associating in any way with for-profit lobbying efforts. That seems draconian, no doubt. The current law provides a cooling off period for members and staff when joining K Street. The problem is that the cooling off period is a joke.

Here's how it works. "Senator Smith" leaves Capitol Hill and joins the "Samson Lobbying Firm." He can't lobby the Senate for two years. But, he can make contact with his former colleagues. He can call them and introduce them to his new lobbying partners, stressing that although he cannot lobby, they can. His former colleagues get the joke, but the joke's on us.

Because the vast majority of lobbyists start on the Hill, this employment advantage is widely exploited. It cannot be slowed with a cooling off period. These folks are human beings, not machines—and human beings are susceptible to corruption and bribery. I should know: I was knee-deep in both. Eliminating the revolving door between Congress and K Street is not the only reform we need to eliminate corruption in our political system. But unless we sever the link between serving the public and cashing in, no other reform will matter.

> "Making ethics reform the first bill of the new Congress is . . . a significant step on the road toward restoring the American people's faith in government."

The Honest Leadership and Open Government Act Provides Unprecedented Ethics Reform

Democratic Policy Committee (DPC)

The Democratic Policy Committee (DPC), recently renamed the Democratic Policy and Communications Committee (DPCC), is an advisory board made up of Senate Democrats that formulates new policy ideas, conducts oversight investigations, and communicates Democratic policies to the public. In the following viewpoint, the DPC comments on the passage of the Honest Leadership and Open Government Act of 2007 (referred to as S. 1). The committee praises the new law for enacting a series of ethics reforms in the Senate regarding the acceptance of gifts and travel, working for lobbying firms, the disclosure of dealings with lobbyists, and the regulation of earmark spending. The legislation

"The Democratic-Led, 110th Congress Delivered a Victory for the American People by Passing Ethics and Lobbying Reform," Democratic Policy Committee (DPC), US Senate, August 3, 2007.

will, the DPC concludes, provide previously nonexistent safe-guards against ethics violations and the strongest punishment to date for fraud or for failing to adhere to the new standards it outlines.

As you read, consider the following questions:

1. According to the Democratic Policy Committee, what types of organizations may still offer paid travel to Congress members under the rules stated in S. 1?

2. How long does S. 1 state that the cooling off period is before a former Congress member may accept a job with a lobbying firm, as reported by the DPC?

3. Under the terms of S. 1, what information must an earmark sponsor submit to the committee of jurisdiction before attaching an earmark request to an appropriations bill, according to the DPC?

The American people are fed up with corruption and abuse in Washington. Faced with the Abramoff scandal [referring to a scandal involving lobbyist Jack Abramoff and Indian casino gambling], criminal indictments, resignations, and the Republican K Street project, 42 percent of voters listed corruption in Washington as the most important factor in determining who they voted for in the last election. Making ethics reform the first bill of the new Congress is—and now passing that legislation in both Houses—a significant step on the road toward restoring the American people's faith in government.

Some Senate Republicans stood in the way of ethics and lobbying reform. In June [2007], one Republican senator, with the support of several members in his caucus, blocked the bill from going to conference with the House of Representatives. Congressional Democrats, disappointed but undeterred, worked to overcome these time-wasting, obstructionist tactics in favor of a bill that would change the way business is done in Washington.

Democrats succeeded in overcoming Republican obstructionism to pass S. 1 [the Honest Leadership and Open Government Act]. Although Democrats wanted to move the House and Senate reform bills through the regular conference process, Republican obstructionism foreclosed that opportunity and forced congressional leaders to pursue other legislative options. In lieu of a conference report, House and Senate Democrats agreed to advance a version of S. 1 that encompassed the reforms of both the House and Senate-passed measures. On July 31 [2007], the House passed that version of S. 1 on overwhelming 411 to 8 vote, and on August 2, the Senate concurred with the House on a vote of 83 to 14. Every Democratic senator voted in favor of this bill, which is now cleared for the president's signature.

Watchdog Groups Praise New Ethics Standards

Washington watchdog groups have consistently praised the Democrat-led Congress's efforts to ensure transparency and accountability in Washington. When the Senate first passed S. 1, Fred Wertheimer, president of Democracy 21, applauded "Senate Democrats for standing firm for this critical ethics and lobbying reform legislation" and expressed his belief that the reforms would "change the way business is done in the Senate." Melanie Sloan, executive director of Citizens for Responsibility and Ethics in Washington (CREW), called the bill "a promising move towards a cleaner Congress" and noted that "Majority Leader Harry Reid and the full Senate deserve credit for passing legislation that tackles many of the ethics issues that plagued the last Congress." Mary Wilson, president of the League of Women Voters (LWV), recognized that "voters . . . expressed a clear dissatisfaction with the unbridled level of corruption in Congress, and . . . passage of ethics and lobbying reform indicates their voices are at last being heard."

"He's Having a Hard Time Letting Go," cartoon by Ed Fischer, www.CartoonStock.com.

After final passage, Democracy 21 president Fred Wertheimer again praised Democrats and noted that this "landmark lobbying and ethics reform legislation is a great victory for the American people."

Limits Will Be Placed on Gifts and Travel

Congress, under Democratic leadership, voted to toughen rules governing gifts and travel. S. 1 will:

- Ban gifts, including de minimis [minor] gifts, from registered lobbyists, agents of a foreign principal, or a private entity that retains or employs a lobbyist or foreign agent;

- Require entertainment and sporting events to be valued at true market value; if a ticket has no face value, it must be valued at the cost of the most expensive ticket;

147

- Prohibit a senator, who is not his/her party's nominee for president, from participating in an event to honor him/her at a national party convention that is directly paid for by a lobbyist or a lobbyist's client.

- Extend the ban on travel paid for by lobbyists or agents of foreign principals to include restrictions on travel paid for by private entities that retain or employ lobbyists or foreign agents (an exception will be made for one-day trips or trips paid for by 501(c)(3) (charitable) organizations);

- Prohibit lobbyists from participating in privately paid congressional travel.

- Require that senators and staff receive approval from the Ethics Committee before accepting expenses for any trip and that, within 30 days, a senator's trips paid for by private sources be disclosed on the Internet; and

- Require members to pay full charter rates for travel on noncommercial planes.

A Cooling Off Period Is Required Before Taking a Lobbyist Job

S. 1 will slow "the revolving door" for former senators and staff. The legislation will:

- Amend the Senate rules and federal conflict of interest law to ban former senior staff (persons making 75 percent of a senator's salary) from lobbying anyone in the Senate for one year, not just his/her former senator or committee;

- Amend conflict of interest law to increase the "cooling off" period, in which former members of Congress are barred from lobbying Congress, from one year to two; and

- Amend conflict of interest law to increase the "cooling off" period for former "very senior" executive branch officials, including cabinet members, from one year to two.

S. 1 will require disclosure of private employment negotiations. The measure will:

- Amend the Senate rules to require a sitting senator to publicly disclose private employment negotiations, until his/her successor has been elected. Irrespective of disclosure, a senator will be prohibited from engaging in negotiations for lobbying-related jobs until after his/her successor has been elected; and

- Require a senior staff member to disclose to the Ethics Committee [the Senate Select Committee on Ethics] employment negotiations and to recuse him/herself from official matters that will create or appear to create a conflict of interest given those negotiations.

S. 1 will prohibit staff contact with lobbyists who are family members of their senator. The legislation will amend the Senate rules to prohibit staff from being lobbied by any member of their senator's immediate family.

Increased Transparency in Lobbyist Dealings

The landmark Democratic reform bill will significantly expand lobbying disclosure requirements related to lobbyists. S. 1 will:

- Require quarterly, rather than semiannually, filing of current disclosure reports;

- Require disclosure of contributions to federal candidates and leadership PACs [political action committees] by lobbyists;

- Require lobbyists to disclose various other contributions made to entities related to senators, presidential libraries, and inaugural committees;

- Require the disclosure of lobbyists' bundled campaign contributions in excess of $15,000 per six months;

- Require registrants to disclose in their registration statements all past executive and congressional employment within the past two decades;

- Increase the civil penalty up to $200,000 for failing to comply with disclosure requirements;

- Increase the criminal penalties, up to 5 years' imprisonment, for knowing and corrupt violations of the Lobbying Disclosure Act (LDA) provisions; and

- Prohibit registered lobbyists from providing gifts or travel to members of Congress or congressional staff that the lobbyist knows will violate congressional rules.

The legislation will also require the creation of a searchable, sortable database that contains information included on LDA disclosure reports.

S. 1 will prohibit partisan efforts like the K Street project. The legislation will amend the Senate rules and federal criminal law to prohibit specifically a senator from threatening to take or withhold official action in order to influence the employment decisions or practices of a private entity solely on the basis of partisan political affiliation.

S. 1 will deny pensions to former members convicted of certain crimes. The legislation will require that members of Congress convicted of bribery or illegal gratuities, or associated crimes, based on acts committed after the effective date, forfeit their federal pension.

S. 1 will protect the integrity of conference reports. The measure will amend the Senate rules to permit a 60-vote point of order against individual items contained in conference reports that have not been committed to the conferees by either legislative body. This legislation will also prohibit consideration of conference reports unless the report had been provided to all senators and made available on the Internet for at least 48 hours.

Tighter Regulation of Earmark Spending

Despite Senate Republican rhetoric to the contrary, S. 1 will also provide the most sweeping transparency to the earmark and legislative process ever enacted. The legislation will amend the Senate rules to create a point of order against a motion to proceed to consideration of a bill, joint resolution, or vote on a conference report if the earmarks and the names of Senate earmark sponsors are not disclosed on the Internet 48 hours in advance. Committee chairmen will be required to identify earmarks and sponsors as soon as possible after the markup of a bill. For a classified earmark, the sponsor's name will also be required in the unclassified language of the measure, along with any descriptive information that does not compromise national security. Earmark disclosure is also required in amendments with earmarks.

For the first time ever, the landmark reform bill will allow any senator to raise a point of order against "new directed spending items" added into conference reports not committed to by the conferees. If the point of order succeeds, the new provision will be struck.

Earmark sponsors will have to submit to the committee of jurisdiction: their name; the purpose of the earmark; for spending earmarks, the name and location of the recipient or activity or for tax or tariff benefit earmarks, the beneficiary; and a certification that neither the member nor his/her immediate family has a pecuniary interest in the earmark.

Further, the bill will amend the Senate rules to prohibit a senator or staff from using his/her official position to work for a congressional earmark that will financially benefit the senator or his/her immediate family member.

S. 1 will also end the Senate practice of secret holds by requiring senators seeking to block a piece of legislation from going forward to identify him/herself within six session days.

| "Some government watchdog groups worry that more and more lobbying activity won't make it into the public record."

The Honest Leadership and Open Government Act Is Ineffective Due to Low Enforcement

Bara Vaida

Bara Vaida reports on Washington, DC, politics—particularly the influence of lobbying—for the National Journal. *In the following viewpoint, she maintains that several factors contribute to the negligible enforcement of the ethics standards outlined in the Honest Leadership and Open Government Act. According to Vaida, these factors include a lack of resources dedicated to investigating infractions, a reluctance by congressional ethics panels to penalize violators, and an inability to monitor what are effectively secret dealings between lawmakers and lobbyists. As a result, she explains, lobbyists and watchdog groups have had to step in and police lobbying activities, as well as force compliance with guidelines.*

As you read, consider the following questions:

1. In Vaida's judgment, how transparent is the ethics review process in Congress?

2. What recent governmental action led many lobbyists to deregister, according to Vaida?

3. What groups does Vaida suggest have been most effective in blowing the whistle on those who commit ethics violations?

Ask any ethics lawyer in Washington what he or she thinks about the enforcement of Congress's lobbying rules and the answer is unanimous.

Chuckling, they say: "What enforcement?"

The numbers tell the story. In the 12 years between passage of the 1995 Lobbying Disclosure Act and 2007, when Congress amended the law, the Senate Office of Public Records and the House Office of the Clerk sent 3,883 potential violations to the U.S. attorney for the District of Columbia, who is charged with enforcing the law. Only three enforcement actions resulted.

In the two years since enactment of the Honest Leadership and Open Government Act, which expanded disclosure of lobbying activities and banned most gifts by lobbyists to lawmakers and staffers, 1,713 potential violations were referred to the U.S. attorney. Zero enforcement actions have been publicly reported. The House and Senate ethics committees oversee the gift ban portion of the lobbying rules. No citations involving lobbyists have been publicly reported by either panel this year [in 2009].

Disclosure Enforcement Is a Low Priority

The apparent lack of action has created the perception that lobbying disclosure enforcement "falls somewhere slightly above jaywalking in priority" for the U.S attorney, said Brett Kappel, of counsel at Vorys, Sater, Seymour and Pease.

In addition to the enforcement concerns, some government watchdog groups worry that more and more lobbying activity won't make it into the public record. Since 2008, 1,800 individuals have de-registered as lobbyists, according to the House Office of the Clerk. The Senate does not estimate de-registrations.

Although lobbyists have many legitimate reasons to de-register (leaving the profession, for example), concern is growing that President [Barack] Obama's expanding list of limitations on registered lobbyists' access to the executive branch is driving some of them to find loopholes. The combination of factors has watchdogs fearing that the stage is being set for new corruption scandals as the case of disgraced lobbyist Jack Abramoff fades from memory.

"If you don't have rigorous enforcement and there is less incentive to disclose lobbying activities, you have a prescription for disaster," said Gary Bass, executive director of OMB Watch. Adds Craig Holman, Public Citizen's legislative representative: "There has to be an attitude change" about enforcing the law.

A handful of staff at the Senate Office of Public Records and the House Office of the Clerk reviews more than 40,000 quarterly disclosure reports to determine if the forms are in order. If an error is found, or if it appears that an organization or lobbyist has stopped filing, the offices give the filer 60 days to address the matter. If there is no response, the case is referred to the U.S. attorney's office for review as a potential violation. Willful violations can result in a $200,000 fine and prison time.

Minimal Resources Are Devoted to Investigation

The Civil Division of the U.S. attorney's office investigates possible violations. Only six employees in its false claims office are tasked to handle lobby reports: two lawyers and four support staffers. And it's a part-time job for all of them because they also work on non-lobby cases. Three lawyers from other offices can be brought in if the workload gets too heavy.

The priority placed on lobbying enforcement "is based on the resources we have," said Keith Morgan, deputy chief of the U.S. attorney's Civil Division. Morgan, who is in charge of the lobbying compliance team, added: "No one is doing this exclusively."

Morgan explained that under the law, the scope of his investigations is limited to referrals of lobbyists who missed reporting deadlines or filled out forms incorrectly. His staff does not dig into the kinds of illegal activities that led to Abramoff's conviction, such as conspiracy to bribe public officials.

This year, the office implemented a computerized system for tracking referrals from Congress and in 2006 installed a phone line dedicated to lobbying oversight. Once the U.S. attorney's office receives referrals, Morgan and his colleagues send compliance letters to the potential violators, giving them the opportunity to correct their filings. Depending on the response and history of the filer, the office may take further action.

"Anecdotally, what I hear is that when a letter goes out from our office, it gets the person's attention," Morgan said. "I get a lot of phone calls and faxes" at that point.

Between December 2007 and January 2009, the U.S. attorney's office sent 768 noncompliance letters to lobbyists, according to the Government Accountability Office [GAO], which sends an annual report to Congress on how the lobbying disclosure law is working. Morgan said that his office sent an additional 40 compliance letters last month. The GAO found that Morgan's staff tagged six lobbyists as repeat offenders, but Morgan declined to say whether enforcement or court actions were filed against them.

Lobbyists Exert Undue Influence on Lawmakers Through Campaign Donations

Legislative lobbying and campaign finance are policed at the federal level by the amended Lobbying Disclosure Act ("LDA") and Federal Election Campaign Act, respectively. The Supreme Court has recognized that each of these activities implicates analogous First Amendment issues, namely, the right to petition the government, freedom of speech, and freedom of association, but has afforded more deference to campaign finance laws while subjecting lobbying regulation to more searching review. Apart from federal regulation that has generally addressed lobbying and campaign finance separately, some states have adopted creative and unique laws aimed primarily at the interaction of lobbying and campaign finance.

Congress recently took its first step toward legislative recognition of the potentially corrupting interplay between these constitutionally protected activities when it passed the Honest Leadership and Open Government Act of 2007 ("HLOGA"). . . . The major issue with respect to these activities . . . is that lobbyists active in campaign finance are in a position to exert undue influence on elected officials above and beyond influence exerted through each activity separately. Because lawmakers already turn to lobbyists on a regular basis for substantive guidance on complex legislation, those lobbyists who contribute large sums to political campaigns can potentially unbalance the democratic process to an extent that justifies substantial limitations on activities that are protected by the First Amendment.

Rand Robins,
"Why the Honest Leadership and Open Government
Act of 2007 Falls Short, and How It Could Be Improved,"
Legislation and Policy Brief, *vol. 2, no. 2, September 24, 2010.*

Watchdog Groups Make Up
for Token Oversight

Unless asked by the House or Senate, Morgan does not investigate people who are lobbying but haven't registered or who de-registered but continue to lobby. (The law spells out several criteria requiring an individual to register, but the key rule applies to those who spend at least 20 percent of their time on lobbying activities and make at least two lobbying contacts during a calendar quarter.)

"There isn't anyone with a green eyeshade here looking at the forms [who] says, 'You lobbied more than you said you did,'" Morgan said. "And there isn't anyone here setting up a video camera on boxes at FedEx Field saying, 'Hey, you had 10 lobbyists in your box and you didn't report it.'"

As a result, it's left to fellow lobbyists or government watchdog groups to blow the whistle on violators. Public Citizen did just that back in 2006 when Tyson Slocum, director of the group's energy division, personally witnessed an employee of Archer Daniels Midland [ADM] lobbying on Capitol Hill but found that the firm hadn't registered to do so. Slocum complained to the company, and ADM registered for the first time.

"If I see your face on Capitol Hill and I notice you aren't registered, then there is a potential violation going on," Holman said.

Whether lobbyists are de-registering to avoid the White House's new influence rules remains an open question. Only a short time ago, there was no downside to signing up to lobby, which led to a lot of "over-registering," said Lisa Gilbert, democracy advocate for the U.S. Public Interest Research Group. She thinks that most individuals who have recently de-registered didn't meet the legal definition in the first place.

But that doesn't mean that Gilbert wouldn't like to see more government enforcement activity.

"We would be highly supportive of increased appropriations to collect the information required [to be] disclosed by HLOGA [Honest Leadership and Open Government Act] from lobbyists," she said. "We, of course, want to see the bill implemented successfully and an effective and transparent disclosure process in place."

In the post-Abramoff era, the majority of lobbyists appear to be on high alert to comply with lobbying disclosure and gift ban rules, because no one wants to go to prison and "the media are looking over their shoulder," Vorys's Kappel said. Explaining lobbying compliance to clients has become a lucrative business for many ethics lawyers in Washington, indicating that people are paying attention to the new rules. In April, the GAO estimated that 94 percent of lobbyists had filled out their forms correctly in 2008.

> *"Neither corporations nor nonprofit groups maintain a monolithic view on policy issues. But when it comes to money and politics, there is no semblance of a level playing field."*

Lobbying and Ethics Legislation Favors Businesses and Undermines Nonprofits' Advocacy Efforts

Larry Ottinger

Larry Ottinger is president of the Center for Lobbying in the Public Interest (CLPI), a nonprofit advocacy group that helps charitable organizations achieve greater effectiveness through the process of lobbying government officials. In the following viewpoint, he maintains that private sector special interest groups have an unfair advantage over nonprofit organizations in their ability to lobby Congress for policy preferences and funding. Ottinger urges foundations to donate more grants to nonprofits for advocacy purposes, recommends that Congress modify the rules for charitable lobbying, and calls upon diverse charitable organizations to unite as one entity to lobby for the common good. Ot-

tinger also concludes that the US Supreme Court's ruling in Citizens United, *which allows unlimited corporate donations to fund election efforts, leaves nonprofits with the financial means little choice but to spend more on lobbying and nonprofits without the financial means at a distinct disadvantage.*

As you read, consider the following questions:

1. According to Ottinger, what was the ratio of spending on federal lobbying between private corporations and nonprofit organizations in 2008?

2. What does Ottinger say charities are prohibited from doing, in addition to making political contributions?

3. In what way can charitable organizations create a stronger, more effective identity, in Ottinger's opinion?

In a nation where large financial interests already dominate public policy, the Supreme Court will probably soon issue a ruling that moves toward allowing businesses and labor unions to spend unlimited funds on partisan political activity.

That action would widen a gulf between nonprofit groups and businesses and could further seriously diminish charities' and foundations' influence, relevance, and clout in shaping solutions to the nation's problems.

To close this gap—and better advance their missions— nonprofit organizations will need the courage to change both the culture and the rules that have held them back from strategic advocacy for far too long.

That will be difficult, because events of the last few decades have undermined public interest advocacy and created a damaging divide between groups that carry out services and those that seek policy changes.

Nonprofits Have Had Little Effect on Policy

Increased reliance by charities on government support, professionalization of the nonprofit world, and both public and private efforts to intimidate charities that seek to promote social change have all done much to keep nonprofit groups away from important public policy debates.

In the business world, the situation is almost exactly the opposite.

With a fiduciary duty to maximize profit for shareholders, large corporate interests increasingly understand that they stand to gain a significant financial rate of return from spending on lobbying and elections.

Indeed, the rates of return for corporations can be staggering. A recently released University of Kansas study shows how large, blue-chip companies successfully spent hundreds of millions of dollars to obtain a 2004 tax holiday that yielded them an average 22,000 percent return on investment on their lobbying and advocacy.

The current disparity between corporate and nonprofit spending in the public policy arena is so large as to represent a difference in kind, not degree. For example, according to a preliminary analysis by the Center for Responsive Politics, corporations spent roughly $3 billion in 2008 on federal lobbying while charitable and social welfare organizations spent an estimated $300 million, a ratio of 10 to 1.

Neither corporations nor nonprofit groups maintain a monolithic view on policy issues. But when it comes to money and politics, there is no semblance of a level playing field.

The Supreme Court Ruling on *Citizens United* Will Reinforce Private Sector Power

This situation is likely to grow even worse given the Supreme Court's expected ruling in *Citizens United v. Federal Election Commission.*

In that case, a majority of the court has signaled its intent to move toward allowing corporations and unions to make unlimited partisan expenditures to elect or defeat specific candidates or political parties. Charities are prohibited not only from making political contributions but also from any partisan political activities.

In a friend-of-the-court brief in *Citizens United*, Independent Sector explains why nonprofit groups should care.

"The influence of money in politics jeopardizes the integrity of the electoral process, impairs the ability of citizens and charitable organizations to exercise their advocacy rights, and discourages participation by individuals and charities," Independent Sector wrote.

Nonprofits Need to Mobilize to Gain Influence

Regardless of how the Supreme Court rules, it is time for charities and foundations to make policy and civic engagement a priority. That means putting time and money into advancing the following ideas.

Foundations must step up their grants for advocacy. Charities want to strengthen their ability to influence public policy, a 2008 survey from the Center for Civil Society Studies at the Johns Hopkins University found. They said money for staff members dedicated to that purpose—as well as increased general operating support from foundations—would best enable them to do so.

But too many foundations are unwilling to make such grants.

According to a new Foundation Center report on grant making from 2002 to 2006, private and community foundations gave approximately 12 percent of their grants to organizations that promote structural changes in how society works. Despite some signs of hope, that 12 percent figure was essentially unchanged from a similar study to examine grant making from 1998 to 2002.

Foundation money is crucial to advocacy. Most government agencies prohibit charities from using any of their money for advocacy, so nonprofit groups must turn to private sources for this work. Some leading organizations have suggested that grant makers earmark as much as 25 percent to 50 percent of their grant dollars to financing advocacy and citizen-involvement efforts.

Simplify the rules. Lack of knowledge, confusion, and fear still dominate the nonprofit world when it comes to advocacy. For example, a study by the Center for Lobbying in the Public Interest, OMB Watch, and Tufts University called "Seen but Not Heard" found that more than one-fourth of charities did not know that they could legally support or oppose federal legislation under current IRS [Internal Revenue Service] rules. In addition, the study found that charities are often reluctant to use the word "lobbying" even when clearly describing lobbying activities.

It is not surprising this is the case, given the tangle of federal rules that nonprofit groups are expected to follow when they seek to influence public policies.

Nonprofit Lobbying Rules Are Too Complicated

Currently, the IRS has two sets of lobbying rules rather than one for most charities; the set that outlines what nonprofit groups can do safely without worrying has not been updated in 30 years.

Several government officials, scholars, and nonprofit leaders have suggested moving to a single system for at least all nonreligious charities, and updating the rules for inflation and how lobbying works.

Nonprofit leaders also are exploring ways to create a bright-line test for charities to use to determine whether they are operating within legal bounds when they run nonpartisan efforts to educate Americans on voting issues and encourage them to vote.

Currently, all the IRS offers is a vague "facts and circumstances" test for such activities that chills nonprofit involvement and undermines the tax agency's work to prevent fraud and abuse in nonprofit politicking.

In addition, charities face another stumbling block because of an executive order on ethics issued by President [Barack] Obama. While the president's order was appropriately aimed at promoting government integrity and the public interest, it instead imposed overly broad and ineffective restrictions on public service by all registered federal lobbyists, including those at charities.

Open Government Benefits Nonprofits

Promote open government. The nonprofit world has a vital stake in promoting democracy and making government effective, responsive, open, and accountable to the broader public.

Common Cause and Public Campaign are leading efforts to change the way congressional campaigns are financed. Under legislation now pending in Congress, the federal government would match the money candidates raise through small donations, with the goal of allowing people of moderate means and the public at large to have more influence of the type now enjoyed by wealthy private donors.

Similarly, nonprofit groups would benefit from other efforts to strengthen democracy, including passage of universal voter registration rules and support for a robust and independent news media that can educate the public and play a watchdog role.

Second, nonprofit organizations as a whole have a shared interest in tax fairness. What's more, they need adequate budgets to fill in the gaps that occur because commercial markets don't have a profit motive to deal with certain issues.

In a political system in which money dominates public policy, wealth inequality leads to political inequality in a reinforcing cycle. As United States Supreme Court Justice Louis

Brandeis remarked, "We can either have democracy in this country or we can have great wealth concentrated in the hands of a few. But we can't have both." Thus, for charities and foundations, reducing poverty is not just about caring for people in need; it is about promoting democracy.

Turn the nonprofit umbrella into a formidable public force. To make involvement in civic affairs an ordinary part of what all organizations do, foundations and charities must forge a stronger nonprofit identity. The legal and moral duty to work for a public purpose defines and differentiates nonprofit groups from for-profit corporations that seek to maximize private gain.

Nonprofits Need to Reorganize

Nevertheless, nonprofit organizations do not identify themselves under one umbrella defined by a commitment to the common good.

Instead, charities are primarily organized by substantive issues such as health, education, or housing or by the city or geographic region where they work.

Some organizations are working to overcome the problems caused by the isolated approaches charities take to political action. The National Council of Nonprofits has coordinated coalitions of charities to fight state budget moves that would hurt charities and the people they serve; Independent Sector has lobbied lawmakers to help them understand that tax credits offered in health-overhaul proposals to help small businesses will not do anything to help nonprofit groups provide health care to their millions of employees because they are tax exempt organizations; and United Way Worldwide includes the word "advocate" in its slogan as it pursues its 10-year goals to improve health, education, and financial stability throughout the nation.

With the current social and economic crises and diminished resources, foundations and charities must increasingly influence public policy if we expect to achieve our missions. It is time for the nonprofit world to finally bridge the service and advocacy gap, and to fully recognize that broad participation in civic life is the foundation of our democracy and of social progress.

> "While the legal complexities of finger food for federal lawmakers have been around for years, new ethics rules for party conventions ... have created a kerfuffle for lobbyists."

Lobbying and Ethics Reform Legislation Confuses and Interferes with Legitimate Political Activities

Randy Furst

Randy Furst is a general assignment reporter at the Minneapolis Star Tribune. *In the following viewpoint, he observes that Congress members have become more cautious about accepting free meals and entertainment from lobbyists and special interest groups due to recently mandated ethics rules. Furst reports that while congressional insiders recognize that these rules were implemented with the best of intentions, they believe that the strict regulations have had a detrimental impact on legitimate business dealings between lawmakers and lobbyists.*

As you read, consider the following questions:

1. According to Furst, how have lawmakers gotten around a rule that prohibits lobbyists from sponsoring parties for individual members of Congress?

2. Why do congressional ethics rules allow members to eat appetizers at lobbyist-sponsored events but not allow them to have sit-down meals with lobbyists, according to Furst?

3. What does Furst state that a Congress member must to do if he or she decides to attend a lobbyist-sponsored event such as a free concert?

When organizers for a party to be held during the Republican National Convention decided they wanted to serve quesadillas, they did what many convention-party menu planners are doing these days:

They called their lawyer.

The legal advice: Quesadillas would be permissible—if they were filled only with cheese. So says Ryan Kelly, who works for Take '08 Events, which is helping to set up the party for what he describes as an "advocacy organization."

So why is cheese OK but chicken or beef problematic? If there was meat on the quesadillas, they might constitute a meal, said Kelly, and under Senate and House ethics rules, members of Congress are forbidden from accepting free meals at many events.

As the Twin Cities [Minneapolis-Saint Paul] gears up for four days of nonstop partying during the Sept. 1–4 [2008] convention, lawyers are working overtime to make sure that politicians will be able to sidle up to a multitude of bars without being put behind them.

While the legal complexities of finger food for federal lawmakers have been around for years, new ethics rules for party conventions were passed by the House and Senate in 2007 as part of a much larger ethics reforms package. The convention rules have created a kerfuffle for lobbyists.

"There is a great deal of confusion about what they can do," said Craig Holman of Public Citizen, a consumer advocacy group based in Washington, D.C. "Some lobbying firms have decided not to go to either of the conventions."

Special memos on the conventions have been issued recently by the House and Senate ethics committees.

A New Party Restriction

One staple of past GOP [Republican] and Democratic conventions was expensive parties put on by lobbying entities that honored individual members of Congress.

The events were criticized by consumer advocates who saw them as a way for corporations to try to buy influence.

The congressional ethics rules adopted in 2007 banned such parties honoring individual members of Congress. But House officials have issued guidelines permitting lobbyists to honor a House delegation or caucus, which has watchdog groups fuming.

"The guideline is absurd," said Fred Wertheimer, president of Democracy 21, a reform group. "It is totally contrary to the ethics rule."

Some lobbyists are shying away from any receptions.

The National Beer Wholesalers Association was among the most active sponsors of gatherings honoring members of Congress at the 2004 Republican convention in New York. But the association is aware of the new ethics rules, and it appears it won't be sponsoring any convention parties. "While we have been active at political conventions in the past, we don't have any plans at this point for the upcoming convention," said Jill Talley, the group's spokeswoman.

A rule that was in place before 2007 prohibits members of Congress and their staffs from accepting meals at invitation-only receptions; they are allowed to eat only food of "nominal value."

However, Congress members can eat free meals at "widely attended events," defined as invitation-only events with 25 or more non-congressional attendees where the event has some connection to the officials' duties.

Still, some convention parties, like AgNite, an after-hours bash, are going to serve only finger food, despite a crowd of 3,000 to 5,000. The sponsor, the Minnesota Agri-Growth Council, wants to avoid even a hint of a violation.

Wieners vs. Wienies

"Heavy hors d'oeuvres qualify as a meal," said Cleta Mitchell, a Washington lawyer. "If you are having a reception, it has to be light appetizers, no forks, just toothpicks."

A wiener, she said, would be prohibited, even on a toothpick. However, a little wienie on a toothpick is fine.

She blames the restrictions on a "pesky little amendment," adding, "I think this is preposterous, frankly, because I don't think it is the genesis of the problem. The people who brought us this whole regulatory regime intend to interrupt the normal social interaction between and among those who do business together."

But reform proponents defend finger food limits. "It might sound a little ridiculous, but the intent was to stop the one-on-one sit-down dinners between a lobbyist and lawmakers which was the trade of currency of Jack Abramoff, who is now in prison for bribing members of Congress," Holman said.

State legislators who are convention delegates must also make sure that they're in compliance with their state laws if they show up at a party held by a lobbying group registered in their state.

Lobbyists Perform a Vital Role in Governments

Despite lobbying's historic identification with corruption of governmental processes, most elected officials readily admit that it would be very difficult, as a practical matter, to conduct the public's business without lobbyists. Lobbyists bring information to officials that they could not otherwise obtain; provide a counterweight to arguments by the executive branch or other interested parties; assist in identifying the consequences of proposed courses of action; and translate into relevant parlance everything from public opinions to demographic data to scientific developments. And the information flows in both directions: Lobbyists interpret for their employers and clients the direction in which Congress may be going on a particular issue, what options remain available with respect to a specific piece of legislation, the potential impact of decisions, and what might be done to affect a desired change in direction. Finally, lobbyists help hold public officials accountable for their actions. These are all good: good for Congress, good for business, and good for the public.

But even if lobbying were not responsible for so many good things, lobbyists and lobbying would still be difficult to control. After all, the First Amendment expressly provides a right "to petition the government for a redress of grievances" and prohibits Congress from making laws that restrict that right—unless, of course, there is an overriding public purpose to be served by a restriction reasonably tailored to attain that goal.

*Thomas M. Susman, "Private Ethics, Public Conduct:
An Essay on Ethical Lobbying, Campaign Contributions,
Reciprocity, and the Public Good,"*
Stanford Law & Policy Review, *vol. 19, no. 1, 2008.*

"In general, under Minnesota law, legislators and constitutional officers cannot take gifts from registered lobbyists," said David Schultz, a professor of public administration at Hamline University.

Politicians also must make sure they do not run afoul of entertainment prohibitions.

For example, Styx, the rock group, will play at AgNite's Sept. 2 reception in Minneapolis. If you are a member of Congress, you might want to stick to the booze and food and skip the free concert or you could be hauled up on an ethics charge. (Casual dinner music is said to be OK.)

At the entrance to the concert room, the Agri-Council will post a notice saying that if you're an official subject to gift laws, you should pay to attend the concert. The charge will be fair market value, which might be in the range of $20 to $40. "We have been working with our [legal] counsel at Faegre & Benson," said Leslie Shuler, the Agri-Council spokesperson.

No Quesadillas, After All

Back to an ingestion question: Would eating lots of finger food turn it into a meal, becoming a violation?

"It is basically on the honor system," Schultz said. "The really bigger issue is not so much whether or not a congressman is going to stuff his face with shrimp on a toothpick." Such receptions, he said, are "an incredibly good opportunity for lobbyists and special interests to really mingle with members of Congress and have serious face time with them."

As for the party planners' quesadilla question: Rather than take any chances, event organizers are scratching the quesadillas and adding calamari on a stick, though the full menu has yet to be finalized.

"When we find out . . . we will have the client's legal counsel review it to make sure everything passes muster," said Kelly of Take '08 Events.

Periodical and Internet Sources Bibliography

The following articles have been selected to supplement the diverse views presented in this chapter.

Kevin Bogardus
"Lobbyists Push Congress to Toughen Rules for Their Industry," TheHill.com, April 9, 2012.

Julie Bykowicz
"Abramoff as Ethics Guru Latest Chapter in Political Second Acts," Bloomberg.com, January 3, 2012.

Cole Deines
"Mysterious Fund Allows Congress to Spend Freely, Despite Earmark Ban," CNN.com, May 28, 2011.

Lee Fang
"Analysis: When a Congressman Becomes a Lobbyist, He Gets a 1,452% Raise (on Average)," RepublicReport.org, March 14, 2012.

Nick Gillespie
"Senatorial Tragedy: 'Without Congressional Earmarks, We Find Ourselves at the Mercy of the Bureaucrats ...,'" Reason.com, April 3, 2012.

Natasha Lennard
"Lobbyists Are Overtaking Congress," Salon.com, July 13, 2011.

Rob Miller
"Three Years After the Honest Leadership and Open Government Act, It's Time to Do More," *Huffington Post*, September 14, 2010.

Ron Nixon
"Congress Appears to Be Trying to Get Around Earmark Ban," *New York Times*, February 5, 2012.

Neil Volz
"Jack Abramoff Exaggerates Congress's Corruption," DailyCaller.com, November 7, 2011.

Jordy Yager
"Tribes Rip Abramoff, Ethics Watchdogs," TheHill.com, March 7, 2012.

OPPOSING
VIEWPOINTS®
SERIES

CHAPTER 4

What Are Some Consequences of Ethics Violations?

Chapter Preface

Signed into law by President Barack Obama on April 4, 2012, the Stop Trading on Congressional Knowledge Act (STOCK Act) prohibits more than twenty-eight thousand high-level employees in the federal government—including members of Congress—from using nonpublic information acquired during the course of their duties for personal financial gain. Specifically, the act states that members of Congress and their staffs are not exempt from federal securities laws prohibiting the insider trading of nonpublic financial information. In addition, senior government officials must post a disclosure of any financial transaction greater than $1,000 involving stocks, bonds, commodities, and so on, on their agency's website within forty-five days of the trade. Previously, officials were required to disclose such transactions only once per year and not always online. The act also authorizes the Government Accountability Office (GAO) and the Congressional Research Service (CRS) to produce a report on the increasing influence of the political intelligence–gathering industry in Washington, DC, and how the brokering of such information can impact financial markets. Other features of the STOCK Act call for the forfeiture of federal pensions for Congress members who are convicted of corruption while serving as elected officials, require legislators to reveal the financial details of personal mortgages, and restrict legislators from participating in initial public offerings that are not open to the general public.

Congressional committees in both the House and Senate debated the key provisions of the STOCK Act for several years prior to its passage into law. Representatives Brian Baird (D-WA) and Louise Slaughter (D-NY) originally introduced it as legislation in the House on March 28, 2006, but it died in committee. Legislators reintroduced the act again in 2007 and

2009, but both times it failed to make it out of committee. In March 2011, Representative Tim Walz (D-MN) yet again introduced the legislation in the House, and it was promptly referred to various committees for further review. When an investigative report into insider trading in Congress aired on the news program *60 Minutes* on November 13, 2011, the pending legislation suddenly captured the full attention of House members, with more than eighty attaching their names to the bill as cosponsors. Within two days of the news report's airing, Senators Scott Brown (R-MA) and Kirsten Gillibrand (D-NY) introduced two versions of the House bill into the Senate for consideration. On January 24, 2012, in his State of the Union address, President Obama increased the political pressure on Congress to pass the legislation, declaring, "Send me a bill that bans insider trading by members of Congress, and I will sign it tomorrow." A Senate version of the STOCK Act passed on February 2, 2012, by a vote of 96–3. On February 9, the House passed its own version of the bill by a vote of 417–2. The Senate endorsed the House version of the legislation with a unanimous vote on March 22, and President Obama signed it into law on April 4.

Insider trading is one of the topics explored in the viewpoints in this chapter, which deals with the debate over what the consequences of ethical lapses by members of Congress are or should be. The authors of the viewpoints explore some highly publicized sexual indiscretions by members of Congress as well as instances in which members have committed criminal acts.

> "The [House] Ethics Committee carries real investigative power, ... but it can't do much in the way of punishment. It can recommend a punishment to the full House, but ... those punishments aren't too severe or meaningful."

Congressional Ethics Committee Investigations Pressure Rather than Punish Politicians

Chris Good

Chris Good is a political reporter for ABC News. Previously, he was an associate editor at the Atlantic *and a reporter for the* Hill. *In the following viewpoint, he maintains that while the House Committee on Ethics lacks the authority to punish House members who commit ethics violations, it can generate enough bad publicity to force the disgraced member to resign on his or her own. Good remarks that neither David Wu nor Anthony Weiner resigned from office as the result of a formal congressional inquiry; rather, both congressmen stepped down after intense media scrutiny and public embarrassment related to their respective sex scandals.*

As you read, consider the following questions:

1. As Good notes, what powers does the House Ethics Committee possess when it comes to dealing with members accused of ethics violations?

2. What historical event caused the most members of Congress to be removed from office, according to Good?

3. What did Democratic House Speaker Nancy Pelosi promise to do following the 2006 elections, as Good reports?

Rep. David Wu, the Oregon Democrat whose mental stability came into question earlier this year [in 2011] after revelations about an incident involving a tiger suit and a 1:00 A.M. e-mail, will now become the latest House Democrat examined by the House Ethics Committee [the House Committee on Ethics].

Wu stands accused of having an "unwanted sexual encounter" with the teenage daughter of a donor and high school friend last Thanksgiving. It's the latest tidbit to emerge about the bizarre period in which Wu started behaving erratically, leading at least six staffers to quit.

The night before last Halloween, Wu sent a photo . . . of himself in a tiger suit to a female staffer just after 1:00 A.M. Pacific, from his congressional Blackberry. Wu was behaving loopily in the final weeks of his sixth congressional reelection campaign, according to news reports. He reportedly had angry outbursts and sent strange e-mails in the voice of his children. Staffers tried to stage two interventions and threatened to shut down his campaign. When the tiger photo surfaced in February, Wu explained the strange behavior by saying he'd taken painkillers given to him by a donor, after leaving his own pills in Washington. The most recent charge has revived reports that Wu was accused of rape in 1976 by a former girlfriend while he was a student at Stanford, but no criminal charges were filed.

Wu will not resign, though he will not run for reelection in 2012 either.

Democrats Receive Ethics Scrutiny

In a letter Monday morning, House Speaker Nancy Pelosi (D-Calif.) formally asked the House Ethics Committee to investigate whether or not Wu broke any laws or House rules. "With deep disappointment and sadness about this situation, I hope that the Ethics Committee will take up this matter," Pelosi said in a public statement e-mailed to reporters.

Wu is now the latest in a string of House Democrats to face formal investigations.

Most recently, Pelosi asked the committee to investigate former congressman Anthony Weiner, another Democrat refusing to resign in the face of a sex scandal. In December, Harlem Democrat Charlie Rangel was censured by the full House after a drawn-out committee investigation into his finances, fund-raising, and backing of a center in Harlem bearing his name. Since 2009 the committee has been investigating Rep. Maxine Waters (D-Calif.) for setting up a meeting between Treasury officials and a bank for which her husband was a board member, as the bank sought bailout money. Last week the committee hired an outside counsel to investigate potential improprieties in its own investigation of Waters, who has asked that the charges against her be thrown out.

The results of an ethics probe aren't always terribly significant. Recently, investigations have functioned more as pressure mechanisms to get a disgraced lawmaker to leave, or as epiphenomena [secondary, accompanying phenomena] indicating that something has gone horribly wrong, in which case the lawmaker in question will usually resign before the Ethics Committee has a chance to release its findings or hold a public hearing, as was the case with Weiner. But it's not the investigation itself that matters, usually.

An investigation into Wu means two things: that Pelosi probably wants him gone, and that he may have done something seriously wrong, the seriousness of which outweighs any formal wrist slaps the House panel can recommend.

The Ethics Committee Has Limited Enforcement Powers

The Ethics Committee carries real investigative power, in that it can subpoena documents and testimony, but it can't do much in the way of punishment. It can recommend a punishment to the full House, but, as we saw in Rangel's case, those punishments aren't too severe or meaningful. The committee recommended a "censure" of Rangel, which was allegedly more serious than a "reprimand," neither of which carried any real consequences. Rangel was ultimately censured by the full House, but, as it turned out, the substance of that punishment entailed . . . the announcement of punishment. The committee can investigate whether any laws were broken, as is commonly requested of it, but it can't file any criminal charges.

Only 20 members have ever been kicked out of Congress, 15 from the Senate and five from the House, the vast majority of whom were Confederate lawmakers who backed secession. Investigations take months, sometimes years, so if Wu did indeed do what he's accused of doing, it's not as if he'll be punished in the near future.

Lawmakers have survived criminal convictions without resigning from Congress. While the present House Ethics Manual requires that members "conduct themselves at all times in a manner that reflects creditably on the House" and "adhere to the broad ethical standards expressed in the Code of Ethics for Government Service," it does not explicitly ban things like nonconsensual sex with teenagers.

The committee's power lies in its ability to surface damning or embarrassing facts, which can prompt criminal investi-

"We have a big pork bill to pass, McFlibley—Would you mind distracting the press with a big sex scandal?," cartoon by Ed Fischer.

gations by the Department of Justice or other law enforcement bodies or, more likely, force a lawmaker from office before the investigation is complete.

Weiner faced an Ethics Committee probe that likely would have found him to have violated House rules by photographing himself nude in the House gym, for the purposes of online flirting. But that wasn't what ultimately forced him out.

Photos Cause Media Sensation

The difference between Wu and Weiner seems to be photographs. Wu has been accused of something arguably much worse than what Weiner admitted to, but only the aforementioned tiger photo exists as tawdry, Internet-friendly evidence. Photos started and then fueled Weiner's story line, before a cyclone of media scrutiny, not the threat of an official censure, ultimately caused him to resign.

Wu's case will change, of course, if more information comes out. His accuser reportedly leveled her claim in a voice mail message, which the committee will be able to obtain. The public will probably not hear it unless it is aired at a public Ethics Committee hearing, a final step in the ethics investigation process that isn't always reached.

A Pelosi aide would not disclose whether or not the House minority leader asked Wu to resign, but it's safe to say Democrats probably won't want him around if the charge is in any way true. Scandalized representatives are bad for party business. House Democrats have a particularly high-profile relationship with ethics issues, as they rose to power in 2006 after a series of GOP [Republican] ethics scandals and the unpopularity of the war in Iraq. Pelosi promised to "drain the swamp," instituting tougher ethics, travel, gift, and lobbying restrictions soon after Democrats took the majority.

Pelosi has not publicly called for Wu's resignation, either, but it won't be surprising to hear her and other lawmakers do so if information surfaces indicating Wu's guilt. Pelosi and others privately urged Weiner to resign and publicly offered those sentiments only after Weiner had not only admitted to online flirtations, but announced he would take a temporary

183

leave from the House, a plan that clearly would not satisfy his critics and many in the public.

In calling for an investigation of Wu, Pelosi sent the thinly veiled message that, if the charge is true, he's not wanted in the halls of Congress. Pressure could mount for his immediate exit depending on what we learn in the coming days and weeks. [Editor's note: Wu resigned on August 3, 2011.]

| "The fact that so many legislators survive scandals suggests that, unless laws are broken or private acts strongly contradict public personas, there is a good chance that a politician can last."

Surviving Sex Scandals

Julian E. Zelizer

Julian E. Zelizer is a professor of history and public affairs at Princeton University. In the following viewpoint, he observes that there is a long history of legislators who became embroiled in sex scandals, and yet they were still reelected to Congress by their constituents. In Zelizer's opinion, voters often will excuse a legislator's personal indiscretions as long as his or her misdeeds are not criminal and as long as the legislator continues to do an effective job of representing the district's interests in Congress. Zelizer concludes that the question that should perhaps be asked about sex scandals involving members of Congress is why they get more coverage in the media than do issues that matter to voters, such as high unemployment.

As you read, consider the following questions:

1. What political aspiration did the 1969 Chappaquiddick scandal prevent Sen. Ted Kennedy from achieving, in Zelizer's judgment?

2. What criminal enterprise managed by an assistant of Rep. Barney Frank led to Frank's reprimand before the House of Representatives in 1990, as Zelizer reports?

3. In Zelizer's opinion, what aspects of a legislator's job performance typically matter more to voters than his or her personal conduct?

Rep. Anthony Weiner (D-N.Y.) has been at the center of a major scandal ever since the conservative web mogul Andrew Breitbart revealed that the congressman's Twitter account was a little more interesting than most. As details about Weiner's tweets and Facebook chats became public, along with photos of naked body parts, the congressman made a profuse public apology.

House Minority Leader Nancy Pelosi (D-Calif.) called for an ethics investigation less than five minutes after he spoke. A growing number of legislators are now demanding that Weiner resign.

Though the pressure has intensified, Weiner insists he is staying in office. A new poll supports his decision—revealing that more than 60 percent of his constituents believe he should not resign.

This is not unusual. Weiner could indeed keep his seat if he can survive the current media storm. Unless legislators violate laws or act in a manner completely contradicting their core public values, voters have proven to be far more forgiving than the media about the foibles of their leaders.

Many legislators involved in sex scandals have preserved their political position. Some have even gone on to have successful careers. It takes an immense amount of pressure to force members into giving up their seats.

Consider the late New York politician and playboy, Rep. Adam Clayton Powell Jr. He was under continual investigation for tax evasion and for misusing public funds to pay for trips with female companions to the Bimini islands. Powell, who represented Harlem, charged that Southern Democrats were attacking him because of his staunch advocacy of civil rights and because he was a powerful African American.

In 1967, the House excluded Powell for technical violations. His constituents reelected him by a 7 to 1 margin in a special election—forcing the case to be decided in the Supreme Court in 1969. Powell regained his seat.

In 1969, Sen. Ted Kennedy was driving a car that veered off a bridge in Chappaquiddick, Mass. The senator escaped, but his passenger, Mary Jo Kopechne, did not. Kennedy didn't report the accident until the following morning.

Many speculated that he panicked for fear that allegations of a relationship with Kopechne would harm his political career. Kennedy went on the offensive. He appeared on national TV to apologize for his irresponsible behavior and to admit that he should have reported the incident immediately. Though the scandal destroyed his presidential aspirations, Kennedy remained the Bay State's senator until his recent death.

It looked like New York Democrat Fred Richmond's career was toast in 1978, when he was arrested for approaching a 16-year-old boy for sexual acts with "payment of money," as he acknowledged. Richmond apologized, admitting that he had not always acted well.

"I cannot offer any logical explanation," Richmond said. "During various periods of personal stress, I made bad judgments involving my personal life."

His constituents reelected him. He resigned within a few years, however, after being caught using drugs and avoiding taxes. But the sex scandal was not the reason.

In the early 1980s, an investigation into rumors of a cocaine ring being run out of Capitol Hill revealed evidence that Massachusetts Rep. Gerry Studds had a relationship with a 17-year-old male page.

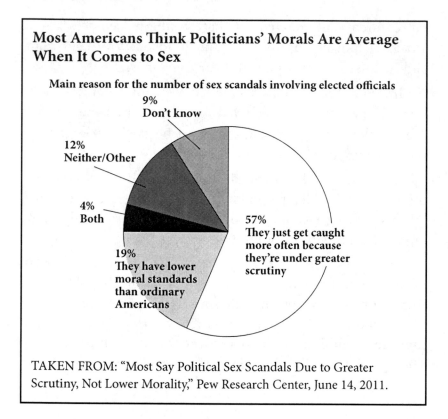

Most Americans Think Politicians' Morals Are Average When It Comes to Sex

Main reason for the number of sex scandals involving elected officials

9%
Don't know

12%
Neither/Other

4%
Both

19%
They have lower moral standards than ordinary Americans

57%
They just get caught more often because they're under greater scrutiny

TAKEN FROM: "Most Say Political Sex Scandals Due to Greater Scrutiny, Not Lower Morality," Pew Research Center, June 14, 2011.

Studds insisted that the relationship was consensual and refused to apologize. The House censured him. But voters did not seem to care. They kept him in office until he left Congress in 1997.

The House reprimanded Rep. Barney Frank (D-Mass.) in 1990, following the discovery that one of his assistants, Stephen Gobie, was running a male prostitution ring out of the congressman's home. Frank had also helped Gobie avoid paying 33 parking tickets.

Frank issued an apology, though he insisted that he had fired Gobie on learning about his business. Not only has Frank been reelected ever since, but he has become an important voice in the Democratic Party.

Virginia Sen. Charles Robb, who first gained national attention when he married President Lyndon B. Johnson's daughter, Lynda, at the White House in 1967, won reelection to the Senate in 1994—despite the fact that NBC broke a story about his relationship with a former Miss Virginia in the 1980s. Robb only admitted to receiving a nude massage from the beauty queen Tai Collins.

In one of the more unusual cases, in 1993, police discovered Rep. Ken Calvert (R-Calif.) in his car having sex with a prostitute. After the police report was released, Calvert insisted that he didn't know the woman was for hire. He told voters about the emotional stress that he faced because of personal matters. Calvert survived his primary—and is still in office.

In 1998, during the drive to impeach President Bill Clinton for lying about a sexual relationship that he had with an intern, Rep. Dan Burton (R-Ind.) admitted to voters that his own life had been far from perfect. He revealed that he had a relationship outside his marriage that resulted in a child.

Voters didn't care. They sent him back to Washington.

More recently, Sen. David Vitter (R-La.) was reelected, though his name appeared in the records of a major Washington escort service.

Voters even overlooked the celebrated 1974 case of Rep. Wilbur Mills, the powerful chairman of the House Ways and Means Committee caught with a stripper, Fanne Foxe, the Argentine Firecracker, who then jumped into the Tidal Basin. The revelation of their relationship—as well as his admission of alcoholism—made front pages across the nation. Yet voters reelected him that November.

Mills did resign after his next term—but only because voters finally turned on him after he made a drunken appearance at Foxe's first striptease show in Boston—a show attended by a room full of reporters.

To be sure, sex scandals have ended congressional careers. Utah Democrat Allan Howe was defeated in 1976, following his arrest for soliciting undercover police, who were pretending to be prostitutes.

That same year, Ohio Democrat Wayne Hays resigned, following stories that his secretary Elizabeth Ray, with whom he had a relationship, was on the public payroll though she couldn't even type.

Mississippi Republican Jon Hinson, a staunch proponent of family values, had survived one scandal, winning reelection in 1980 after admitting to being gay and having been accused of an obscene act a few years earlier. But he resigned in 1981, after being arrested for sodomy with a man who worked in the Library of Congress.

In 1982, Illinois Republican Dan Crane, who admitted to a relationship with a 17-year-old female page as a result of page-gate, didn't win reelection. The socially conservative Maryland Republican Robert Bauman, after the discovery that he had sexual relations with a 16-year-old boy, was also defeated for reelection.

House Speaker Newt Gingrich was forced to step down from his leadership position because of his own affair—which took place in the middle of the impeachment proceedings against President Bill Clinton. This happened after the poor showing by Republicans in the 1998 midterms, but it demonstrated that sex can matter.

Yet the fact that so many legislators survive scandals suggests that, unless laws are broken or private acts strongly contradict public personas, there is a good chance that a politician can last as long as the pressure of the scandal doesn't compel them to resign.

The reason is that the personal life of a legislator is not always the main criteria by which Americans judge their leaders. Certainly, many people enjoy following the salacious details of these stories. But at the ballot box, voters support legislators who can take care of their states and districts, champion local causes and take the time to develop strong relationships with their electorate.

U.S. voters may be more European in their thinking than we care to admit—willing to forgive politicians for serious personal indiscretions.

Perhaps the real scandal isn't Weiner. Not that his activities were judicious or irrelevant. But perhaps the question is why the media and the public have devoted so much attention and space to Weiner's tweets and chats—rather than the big problem that concerns most Americans, like, for example, the causes behind the stunningly high unemployment rate.

In the end, this issue is likely to matter far more to the average voter than what Weiner tweeted.

> *"Sex over phone lines or the Internet introduces a new layer of potential exposure for members of Congress and ambiguity about how the institution should respond to it."*

Sex Scandals in Congress: What Rep. Weiner's 'Sexting' Adds to the Literature

Gail Russell Chaddock

Gail Russell Chaddock is a staff writer for the Christian Science Monitor. *In the following viewpoint, she maintains that the "sexting" scandal involving Rep. Anthony Weiner (D-NY) raises intriguing new questions about how to proceed with the investigation of congressional ethics violations in the digital age. Chaddock observes that ethics standards are somewhat ambiguous when an offender uses an official Internet-accessible congressional resource—such as a social media application, a Blackberry phone, or even a wireless network—to perpetrate their unethical behavior. Chaddock also asserts that while sexual conduct was once considered a private matter, standards have become stricter over the years, and the potential for public exposure via electronic media has raised the stakes considerably.*

As you read, consider the following questions:

1. Why have Congress members been reluctant to set an ethical standard with regard to sexual conduct, according to Chaddock?

2. What sex scandal do Republican leaders believe caused them to lose control of Congress in the 2006 elections, as Chaddock reports?

3. In Chaddock's opinion, what potential ethical violation do congressional leaders believe is more serious than a member getting caught up in a sex scandal?

Congress has never had a consistent line on the sexual missteps of its members, and the "sexting" done by Rep. Anthony Weiner (D) of New York is adding new twists to a tangle of precedents.

At issue, as in all ethics cases, is whether a member "behave[s] at all times in a manner that shall reflect creditably on the House"—the golden rule of the House's Code of Official Conduct.

But the definition of what behavior fails that standard, especially in matters relating to sex, has shifted over time.

Until the 1980s, all but the most notorious sex scandals were viewed as a private matter, between lawmakers and their families or voters. Moreover, a culture of heavy drinking—much less evident today—was widely accepted both in Congress and within the press corps that covered it.

Both then and now, lawmakers have been reluctant to set a standard on sexual behavior that many members could potentially fail—or that could encourage witch hunts.

"It's a risky standard for members if every time someone engaged in sexually inappropriate conduct, they are going to have to leave Congress," says Melanie Sloan, executive director of Citizens for Responsibility and Ethics in Washington (CREW), a government watchdog. "Sexual conduct per se is not an ethics violation."

But exceptions to this no-fault culture have emerged over time. And sex over phone lines or the Internet introduces a new layer of potential exposure for members of Congress and ambiguity about how the institution should respond to it.

"Most of the sex scandals of the past involved going to a motel and sneaking around," says Ray Smock, a former House historian who directs the Robert C. Byrd Center for Legislative Studies in Shepherdstown, W.Va. "This electronic stuff is uncharted water."

The Stripper and the Committee Chairman

The first modern congressional sex scandal with public consequences dates to a late-night incident in October 1974. It involved stripper Fanne Foxe, who leapt into Washington's Tidal Basin and was rescued by police, and Rep. Wilbur Mills (D) of Arkansas, the powerful chair of the House Ways and Means Committee. The incident hit the front pages. A subsequent appearance with "the Argentine firecracker" on a burlesque stage kept this narrative of bizarre behavior alive. Mr. Mills resigned his chairmanship that December, citing alcoholism, and did not seek reelection in 1976. He never faced a formal investigation by his House peers.

The same year, the House took no action against Rep. John Young (D) of Texas, after an aide charged that she had been put on the payroll primarily for sex, or against Reps. Joe Waggonner (D) of Louisiana or Allan Howe (D) of Utah, who were arrested after soliciting police decoys who were posing as prostitutes.

By the 1980s, the House, along with the general public, began to take sexual misdeeds more seriously. Reps. Gerry Studds (D) of Massachusetts and Daniel Crane (R) of Illinois were both censured by the House in 1983 for sexual relations with

Standards for Online Conduct Are Not Clearly Understood

If politicians recognize that they can't get away with hard drinking and carousing in public, some have simply found new outlets for bad behavior online. They may understand that they cannot be seen leaving a party with a lobbyist of the opposite sex, but sending raunchy pictures online at midnight seems somehow different.

Kate Zernike, "Naked Hubris: Technology and the Political Sex Scandal," New York Times, June 11, 2011.

teenage congressional pages. Mr. Studds went on to serve 14 years, but Mr. Crane was defeated in the next election.

In recent years, harassment of younger staff has evolved into a swift ticket out of Congress for lawmakers on both sides of the aisle. In September 2006, Rep. Mark Foley (R) of Florida resigned his seat 10 days after reports of sending sexually explicit computer messages to former congressional pages. In March 2010, Rep. Eric Massa (D) of New York resigned a month after allegations of harassment and groping of younger staff.

GOP [Republican] leaders still cite the Foley scandal as contributing to the loss of their House and Senate majorities in the 2006 midterm elections.

The Perks of Congressional Office

The current speaker, John Boehner (R) of Ohio, has declared "zero tolerance" for scandal. After Feb. 9 disclosures that Rep. Christopher Lee (R) of New York, who is married, had sent shirtless photos of himself via a dating website, he turned in his resignation to Mr. Boehner the same day.

Another element that elevates sex to an actionable issue for a member of Congress is evidence of abuse of office. For most of congressional history, a sex scandal alone wasn't enough to end a congressional career. But a sex scandal plus evidence that a lawmaker used the perks of congressional office is viewed on both sides of the aisle as a more serious offense.

After Elizabeth Ray, a secretary on the House Administration Committee, famously told reporters in 1976 that her $14,000 a year job was in exchange for sex—"I can't type. I can't file. I can't even answer the phone"—Rep. Wayne Hays (D) of Ohio's days as chairman were numbered. Under pressure from House Democratic leaders, Hays resigned as chair and announced that he would not run for reelection.

House Democrats are using the Hays precedent as a template for responding to the public uproar over the Weiner "sexting" disclosures. No one has denounced sending sexually explicit images or messages per se—a position that potentially opens up all members to scrutiny of e-mail and text messages. Instead, House Democratic leader Nancy Pelosi on Monday called for an investigation "to determine whether any official resources were used or any other violation of House rules occurred."

On Tuesday, she sent a formal request to the House ethics panel to determine "whether the rules of the House of Representatives" have been violated.

Were Official Resources Used?

In his press conference on Monday, Congressman Weiner responded to concerns over whether his "inappropriate conversations conducted over Twitter, Facebook, e-mail, and occasionally over the phone" involved the use of official resources. He said that he used his personal BlackBerry and home computer.

"I don't have knowledge of every last communication but I don't believe that I used any government resources," he said.

Asked whether he conducted any of these exchanges on congressional time, he responded: "Congressional time could theoretically be anything.

Congressmen work long hours. But I don't believe I did anything here that violates any law or violates my oath to my constituents."

He also dispensed with a defense of choice in many congressional sex scandals. "I don't do drugs. I was not drinking," he added.

House rules allow "incidental use" of equipment owned, leased, or reimbursed by the House of Representatives, provided such use is "negligible in nature, frequency, time consumed, and expense," according to the members' congressional handbook.

"For example, limited use of government resources to access the Internet, to send or receive personal e-mail, or to make personal phone calls is permissible, so long as the use meets the above criteria, and otherwise conforms with the regulations of the Committee on House Administration and the Code of Official Conduct," including the standard of conduct that reflects "creditably on the House."

"The regulations dictate what the content must conform to as well as the use of official equipment," says Salley Wood, director of communications for the House Administration Committee.

What About Wi-Fi?

A new issue raised by the Weiner investigation is whether use of the House Wi-Fi system also constitutes use of official resources. If, for example, a member sent an e-mail from a personal Hotmail account but was using the office Wi-Fi, it would go out with an IP (Internet protocol) address through the House server, just as if the member were using a computer hardwired to the office Internet. "That's an issue that has never come up," says spokeswoman Wood.

Another issue potentially involving the use of official resources is whether Weiner volunteered the use of his congressional staff when he volunteered to help one of his correspondents field questions from the news media. If so, it's a violation of House rules. "My staff has never had any contact with her," Weiner said on Monday. "My staff did not know the actual story here. I misled them as well."

Meanwhile, congressional Democrats are keeping their distance from Weiner and his woes. On Tuesday, Senate Majority Leader Harry Reid told reporters: "I know Congressman Weiner. I wish I could defend him, but I can't." Asked what he would say if Weiner asked for his advice, Reid said: "Call somebody else."

"It's very fair to say that the leadership is furious about how he's handled this," said a senior Democratic aide. "The letter that [Pelosi] has now written [to the House ethics panel] certainly adds to the pressure for him to go. Some of it may be dependent on the next thing to come out."

> "While your 401(k) and all thoughts of retirement melted into a never-ending job at Walmart, the House chairman made a tidy profit on his country's misfortunes. And he didn't do anything illegal."

Insider Trading Is Unethical and Calls for Strict Regulation and Harsh Punishment

Jim Galloway

Jim Galloway writes a blog called Political Insider *for the Atlanta Journal-Constitution. In the following viewpoint, he asserts that Congress members often have exclusive access to financial information that gives them a distinct advantage over the average investor when it comes to buying or selling investments. While practicing such insider trading is not illegal, Galloway remarks, it is unethical. He observes that Congress is taking steps toward regulating such behavior by introducing legislation that would prohibit lawmakers and their staffers from profiting from nonpublic financial information.*

As you read, consider the following questions:

1. What financial experts did senators outperform when it came to picking investments, according to a report cited by Galloway?

2. By how many percentage points did senators beat the financial market from 1993 to 1998, as the report cited by Galloway indicates?

3. In Galloway's opinion, why will the implementation of a financial disclosure system in Congress not adequately address the problem of insider trading?

Whether you are Republican or Democrat, an occupier [a member of the Occupy Wall Street movement] or a tea partyist, the report last Sunday [November 13, 2011] by CBS's *60 Minutes* on insider trading by members of Congress should have steam whistling from your ears.

But there's more to tell. And the news will not make you any happier.

The most egregious example cited by CBS was U.S. Rep. Spencer Bachus of Alabama, who three years ago was the ranking Republican on the House banking committee, and is now its chairman.

In September 2008, Bachus and other congressional leaders were privately briefed by Treasury secretary Hank Paulson and Federal Reserve chairman Ben Bernanke on the economy's imminent meltdown.

The next day, Bachus was buying option funds that would increase in value if the economy tanked. It did. While your 401(k) and all thoughts of retirement melted into a never-ending job at Walmart, the House chairman made a tidy profit on his country's misfortunes.

And he didn't do anything illegal.

Financial investments by House Speaker John Boehner and former Speaker Nancy Pelosi also earned mentions. And yet, there is the temptation to write such incidents off as exceptions that prove the rule of good behavior.

Congress Members Have Been Trading Inside Information for Years

But in fact, the insider trading problem in Congress is systemic and long-standing. Though it received no mention, the foundation of the *60 Minutes* report was 16 years of analysis by an academic quartet led by Alan Ziobrowski, a professor of real estate finance at Georgia State University.

His wife, Augusta State University professor Brigitte [J.] Ziobrowski, James Boyd of Lindenwood University and Ping Cheng of Florida Atlantic University served as fellow researchers—as did an army of grad students.

"For years, we went through financial disclosure forms and we digitized their stock transactions. And then we ran a series of tests to see how [members of Congress] compared to the market," Alan [J.] Ziobrowski said this week [in November 2011].

"The bottom line was that they considerably beat the market. In academic finance, we consider that to be prima facie evidence of insider trading," he said. "They were even better than corporate insiders at it." Senators were the best and even outperformed hedge fund managers.

Technically, Ziobrowski said, what members of Congress (and their staffers, one presumes) are engaged in isn't insider trading. That's a term reserved for executives within a particular corporation.

Congress Members Have Access to the Best Trading Information

"What we claim they have is an informational advantage," he said. "These guys have information that's outside the corporation. Probably, companies would love to know what they know."

Insider Trading Is the Norm in Congress

Congress makes decisions that affect the stock market, and members often are privy to information affecting stock prices before the general public. In the corporate world, trading on such information is called insider trading. In Congress, it is business as usual.

Studies have documented how members of Congress have a much higher rate of return on their investments than the average Joe. A new book that documents congressional insider trading in detail breathed new life into the issue this past November [2011] and triggered a *60 Minutes* exposé on the topic. The broadcast profiled several members of Congress who profited from investments after discovering inside information. Rep. Spencer Bachus (R-AL), for example, bought securities that would profit if the market tanked the day after meeting secretly with the Treasury secretary and Federal Reserve chairman. Rep. Bachus sold the securities less than a week later, nearly doubling his money.

"Top Scandals 2011," Citizens for Responsibility and Ethics in Washington (CREW), 2011.

Little things like regulations that can be added or subtracted, defense spending that might be cut or increased. That sort of thing.

The Ziobrowski crew has eschewed anything that might smack of partisanship—which explains its absence from the *60 Minutes* report.

A first study, covering investments of U.S. senators from 1993 to 1998, was published in 2004. A second, larger study took the measure of 16,000 stock transactions by U.S. House members from 1985 to 2001. It was just published this spring in an academic journal, with this priceless title: "Abnormal Returns from the Common Stock Investments of Members of the U.S. House of Representatives."

Partisan differences in investment returns were minimal. Senators beat the market by 12 percent per year, House members by 6 percent—a difference that could be explained by the fact that the Senate is a smaller club, where access to fruitful information is more concentrated.

In the House, younger members made greater gains in the market than senior members. Possibly because younger members are less financially secure and more likely to take financial risks.

Congress Members Cannot Fight the Temptation to Use Inside Information

A large part of me wants to believe that members of Congress are simply brighter than the rest of us, perhaps more aware of societal and financial trends. It is a sliver of hope that Ziobrowski politely demolishes.

"From my perspective, it's fairly simple. If I'm sitting on a pile of $50,000 worth of stock of XYZ Company, and I find out that something's coming down the pike that's not going to be good for XYZ, how could you resist the temptation to unload it?" he asked.

Democrats and Republicans have introduced legislation this week to prohibit members of Congress and their staffs from using nonpublic information for investing or personal gain. Investment transactions would have to be reported within 90 days.

Ziobrowski said the legislation would be better than nothing. "The problem is the system is rigged. The whole notion that, somehow, financial disclosure solves all the ethical issues is really quite a joke. Financial disclosures are not audited. There's nobody to check them to see if they're accurate. Even if they are accurate, the public doesn't see them for a year, year-and-a-half after the transactions have been made," he said.

Corporate insiders are required to report their stock transactions immediately. Ziobrowski would like to see Congress adopt that rule. Though there's no chance that it will.

But the House-Senate "super committee" in charge of formulating a deficit reduction deal has a deadline coming up next week. The impact on your economic fortune and mine may hang in the balance.

It sure would be nice to know if any members of Congress are saying the right things in public—and betting against us in private.

> "It's hard to believe that the mass of pro-
> fessional and amateur investors are
> continually outsmarted by shrewd
> Washington insiders."

Strict Regulation of Congressional Insider Trading Is Misguided and Unnecessary

Daniel Gross

Daniel Gross is a financial columnist who has contributed ar-
ticles to Slate, Newsweek, *and* Yahoo Finance. *In the following*
viewpoint, he questions the need for the passage of a 2007 bill
entitled the Stop Trading on Congressional Knowledge Act
(STOCK Act). Gross contends that just because an investor pos-
sesses prior knowledge of a congressional action that might influ-
ence the financial markets does not guarantee that the markets
will respond as the investor predicts. Gross also suggests that any
legislation that attempts to regulate the flow of information
could be unconstitutional.

As you read, consider the following questions:

1. What are the two principal goals of the proposed Stop Trading on Congressional Knowledge (STOCK) legislation, according to Gross?

2. How does Gross distinguish between acting on nonpublic congressional information and engaging in insider trading in the financial industry?

3. In Gross's judgment, what kinds of organizations would be affected if Congress were to regulate access to political intelligence?

Alert! Apparently, people in Washington are trying to make money by trading on information about the legislative process. To end such shocking, shocking activities, Rep. Brian Baird, D-Wash., and Rep. Louise Slaughter, D-N.Y., last week [in May 2007] introduced the "Stop Trading on Congressional Knowledge Act, or STOCK Act." The goal is twofold: (1) to make it illegal for congressional and federal workers to use knowledge gleaned on the job to trade stocks; and (2) to regulate "political intelligence" research shops, which essentially gather information from Capitol Hill and retail it to hedge funds and other money managers.

Given all the problems that demand congressional oversight and activity—the subprime lending mess, Iraq, the Justice Department—it's difficult to see why this far-reaching legislation, which would direct the Securities and Exchange Commission [SEC] to punish violators, is necessary. Yes, it's absurd that it's apparently legal for junior staffers and members of Congress to day-trade from their Capitol Hill offices based on knowledge of a speech a senator will give tomorrow. And, yes, isolated news accounts—i.e., that Tom DeLay staffer Tony Rudy was doing a lot of day-trading out of the then speaker's office and that buildings-supply company USG [United States Gypsum Corporation] saw its stock rise ahead of a 2005 speech by then Senate Majority Leader Bill Frist about the potential creation of an asbestos trust fund—have engendered suspicions. So too has academic research such as this 2004 paper ["Abnormal Returns from the Common Stock Investments of the U.S. Senate"], which found that senators' investments chalked up abnormally high returns and concluded "senators trade with a substantial informational advantage."

But the evidence isn't fully convincing. It's hard to believe that the mass of professional and amateur investors are continually outsmarted by shrewd Washington insiders. (It could be, for example, that senators' investments did abnormally well in the 1990s because good brokers and money managers were eager for their business.) Any concern that senators are slinging stocks could be allayed through a system of more or less instant disclosure of trading activity. (Voters would thus have the opportunity not merely to support Sen. Hillary Clinton but to trade alongside her.)

Congressional Inside Information Is Not a Sure Thing

Even if Capitol Hill is plagued by widespread trading based on a perceived informational edge, it doesn't require the same sort of insider-trading charges that are filed against Wall Street malfeasants. Defined by the SEC, insider trading occurs when people act on access to material, nonpublic data relating to a regulated company. If an insider at Company X gets wind of an impending takeover for $45 a share from Company Y, he knows that he will certainly be able to profit based on the trading. In insider trading, the connection is direct, and the profit is sure.

But with legislation, the link between advanced knowledge of a senator's position on an issue and the certainty that a specific stock will benefit as a result is much more tenuous. Sure, activity in Washington has the potential to affect compa-

Financial Disclosure Reports Encourage Congressional Transparency

To restrain members from taking personal advantage of nonpublic information and using their positions for personal gain, Congress has decided that such unethical behavior is best discouraged by the public disclosure of financial investments by representatives and the discipline of the electoral process. Each year, every member of the House is required to submit a financial disclosure report (FDR) which identifies all common stock purchases or sales made by the representative, the representative's spouse and their dependent children during the previous calendar year, provides the dates of the transactions, and indicates the approximate value of the transactions. Such disclosures are intended to provide the electorate with the necessary information to judge the representatives' official conduct in light of their private financial interests. . . .

Both the financial disclosure reports (FDRs) and congressional voting records are available to the public. FDRs, submitted annually by House members, are printed, bound together typically in two or three large volumes, and are sent to federal document depositories throughout the country. Some FDRs can also be examined on the websites of private "government watchdog" groups. Voting records are officially available in the *Congressional Record*, which is likewise printed and sent to federal document depositories. Voting records are also available online at various websites.

Alan J. Ziobrowski, James W. Boyd,
Ping Cheng, Brigitte J. Ziobrowski, "Abnormal Returns
from the Common Stock Investments of Members
of the U.S. House of Representatives,"
Business and Politics, *vol. 13, no. 1, 2011.*

nies, sectors, and entire markets—the Federal Reserve moving interest rates, the Food and Drug Administration rejecting a pharmaceutical application, the Pentagon placing an order for jet fighters. Advance knowledge of a congressional speech by the majority leader proposing an asbestos trust fund can certainly move a stock. But it might not. The *Wall Street Journal* noted that back in 2005, "the stock prices of some companies that used asbestos, including USG Corp., W.R. Grace & Co. and Crown Holdings Inc., went up in the two days prior to the senator's announcement. The stock prices of other companies in their sectors were fairly flat on those days." And just because language is included in a speech or in a bill doesn't mean a company can count on the benefits. A lot of things can happen: Multiple committees weigh in; there's the possibility of a filibuster or a veto. (Nothing ever came of that Frist-proposed asbestos trust fund, by the way.) Unless he's a brilliant trader, a Hill staffer who buys options today on a company that he thinks might benefit from something his boss might say next week will have a tough time profiting.

The STOCK Act Undermines First Amendment Rights

The STOCK Act also takes a curious swipe at the First Amendment with its attempt to regulate so-called political intelligence firms, which, Baird and Slaughter say, "provide investors with inside information about impending legislative action that can be used to inform investment decisions." They want to require firms in this industry "to register with the House and Senate, much like lobbying firms are now required to do."

Again, a probably harmless idea. But who, precisely, is in the "political intelligence" industry? Think about all the professionals who make their living peddling information about what goes on in Washington: law firms, consultants like this guy, lobbyists, and researchers pitching glorified tip sheets to investors. Oh, and news organizations. The "political intelligence" shops aren't doing anything much different than, say, the *Washington Post, National Journal,* or the *Wall Street Journal.* After all, these companies employ Washington-based operatives who spend their days working government contacts to unearth information that isn't available to the public. The companies then sell that information exclusively to people who feel that knowledge of such information is important to their businesses. Will *Slate's* crack Washington bureau staffers be required to register as well?

> "[Mark] Twain and the jury [in the Tom DeLay trial] put the blame for the criminalization of politics where it belongs: on the political leaders who sell their favors."

DeLay's Guilty Verdict a Comment on Politics

Rick Casey

Rick Casey is a reporter for the Houston Chronicle. *In the following viewpoint, he comments on the circumstances surrounding former US House member Tom DeLay's trial and conviction for federal money laundering in 2010. According to Casey, DeLay's claim that he is an innocent victim of a political witch hunt is a pathetic defense. In fact, Casey argues, DeLay's involvement in the Texas redistricting scheme that eventually led to his arrest and conviction was so corrupt and so brazen that he ultimately lost the confidence of some fellow Republican legislators.*

As you read, consider the following questions:

1. According to Casey, what does Mark Twain say is America's only criminal class in his book *Following the Equator*?

2. What are Texas's two simple rules when it comes to making political donations, as Casey reports?

3. Why did Tom DeLay think that a jury made up mostly of Democratic and independent voters would acquit him of money laundering charges, as Casey points out?

Justice partnered with farce and pathos last week when a jury, after 19 hours of earnest deliberation, found Tom De-Lay guilty of felony money laundering.

When DeLay was indicted a little more than five years ago, he was one of the most powerful men in the world.

Now DeLay is a fading symbol of the excesses of power, more famous for his game but embarrassing performance on *Dancing with the Star*(let)*s* than for his former role as chief enforcer of the Republican power structure, a man so powerful and ruthless that he could require large lobbying firms to purge themselves of Democratic partners.

DeLay responded to the jury's verdict by arguing, farcically and pathetically, that he was an innocent victim of forces so big that they threaten the Republic.

"The criminalization of politics undermines our very system, and I'm very disappointed in the outcome," he said.

Politics has been criminalized, but it's not exactly a recent phenomenon and he is not exactly a victim.

Mark Twain remarked on it five score and 13 years ago in *Following the Equator*.

"It could probably be shown by facts and figures," Twain wrote, "that there is no distinctly native American criminal class except Congress."

Twain and the jury put the blame for the criminalization of politics where it belongs: on the political leaders who sell their favors.

Politicians do their best to skirt what few anti-corruption laws they or their predecessors have passed in response to the public pressure that occasionally erupts in response to history's

DeLay's Downfall Is a Sobering Lesson to Politicians

For the new class of Republican leadership in Washington headed by [Representative] John Boehner ... and Senator Mitch McConnell, the downfall of DeLay offers many a sobering lesson. Boehner has promised to run a more open-door House with less of the shadowy deal making that DeLay and his allies so excelled in. To every politician in the US it is a reminder that the line between creative use of donations and breaking the law is a thin one.

David Usborne,
"Why the Republicans' Hammer Got Nailed,"
Independent *(London), November 26, 2010.*

perpetual parade of political scandals. There are plenty of generous loopholes through which they can find cover.

Texas has only two simple strictures on the marketplace of buying politicians.

The first is that while there is no limit to how much a patron can give to the politician, it must be a public transaction.

The second is that corporations and unions can't directly give money to candidates.

These are not exactly onerous restrictions. Texas politicians, both Republican and Democrat, have received contributions of more than $1 million from individuals with obvious interests, putting ordinary citizens at a crippling disadvantage in influencing our government.

An Inconvenience

Yet DeLay considered these bedrock rules to be a mere inconvenience, showing the same spirit that famously inspired his response to being told at the height of his power that he couldn't smoke in a Washington restaurant because of federal law.

"I am the federal government," he said.

So he used his position as majority leader to rake in big bucks from corporations all over the country who wanted his help on federal bills.

Then he and a few cohorts took $190,000 of that corporate money, gave it to the Republican National Committee, which then sent exactly $190,000 to a list of candidates for the Texas House of Representatives that DeLay's people provided.

The money was targeted to candidates who agreed to support Rep. Tom Craddick to become the first Republican speaker of the Texas House. Craddick, in turn, committed to DeLay's plan of redrawing the state's congressional districts to design more of them for Republicans—just two years after their normal once-a-decade redrawing.

It Changed Austin

It worked, but one by-product may constitute DeLay's most serious crime.

The bitter process moved the legislature a large step toward making Austin as destructively hyper-partisan as Washington. (Some House Republicans were so offended by this horror that last year they broke ranks and joined Democrats in electing Rep. Joe Straus to replace Craddick, based on his promise to return civility to the Capitol, a promise he has kept.)

One of the more amusing moments of DeLay's trial, to me, came when the jurors during deliberations sent a note to the judge asking if it was illegal to ignore the purpose for which donors gave money.

It's not as though the companies that gave DeLay's Texans for a Republican Majority PAC wanted it used for polio research and he was spending it on private school scholarships.

When Westar Energy Inc. of Topeka, Kan., gave $25,000, its interest was laid out in an e-mail from its lobbyist to a company executive: "(DeLay's) agreement is necessary before the House conferees can push the language we have in place in the House bill."

Voted with Empathy

The donors didn't care what DeLay did with their money. They just cared what he did for them. Another amusing moment came when DeLay told reporters while the jury was out that he was comfortable with the panel's makeup of a Republican, six Democrats, two independent conservatives and three independent liberals, including a Greenpeace activist as forewoman.

DeLay said he was putting his faith of acquittal with the liberals because they were more empathetic, reported my colleague R.G. Ratcliffe.

"I know them like they're my brothers and sisters," DeLay said.

DeLay's former Republican colleagues didn't want empathy in a Supreme Court justice. But when you're the defendant, empathy in the justice system doesn't seem like such a bad idea.

The jurors haven't spoken publicly yet, but I believe they voted their empathy—empathy for those who would like to have a government of the people, by the people and for the people.

And who don't agree with the U.S. Supreme Court that corporations are people.

Periodical and Internet Sources Bibliography

The following articles have been selected to supplement the diverse views presented in this chapter.

Jonathan Allen	"Eric Cantor Smacks Down 'Insider' Spencer Bachus," Politico.com, December 8, 2011.
John Bresnahan	"Ethics Still Reviewing Rep. Shelley Berkley," Politico.com, March 23, 2012.
Dan Eggen	"Congressional Investigators Find 'Reason to Believe' Buchanan Broke Ethics Laws," *Washington Post*, February 6, 2012.
Roderick M. Hills and Harvey L. Pitt	"The Politics of Congressional Ethics," *Gadsden Times* (Alabama), March 8, 2012.
Mike Lillis and Russell Berman	"Insider Trading Ban Gains Momentum, Pelosi Backs House Version of Bill," TheHill.com, December 1, 2011.
Megan McArdle	"Capitol Gains," *Atlantic*, November 2011.
Roger Runningen and Derek Wallbank	"Obama Signs Ban on Congressional Insider Stock Trading," Bloomberg.com, April 4, 2012.
Sheryl Gay Stolberg	"When It Comes to Scandal, Girls Won't Be Boys," *New York Times*, June 11, 2011.
Jeremy Wallace	"Federal Inquiry Focuses on Buchanan," *Herald-Tribune* (Sarasota, FL), October 19, 2011.
Deirdre Walsh	"Obama Signs STOCK Act to Address 'Deficit of Trust' in Washington," CNN.com, April 4, 2012.
Grace Wyler	"More Insider Trading Deals: Here's How Rep. Spencer Bachus Cashed In on the Financial Crisis," *Business Insider*, November 14, 2011.

For Further Discussion

Chapter 1

1. Do the viewpoints provided by Mark Hemingway and Donald Lambro reflect optimism or skepticism toward the ethical oversight process in Congress? How do Hemingway's and Lambro's opinions differ from those of Paul Blumenthal? Explain.

2. The opinions expressed by Citizens for Responsibility and Ethics in Washington and John Bresnahan illustrate two strikingly different perspectives on the effectiveness of the Office of Congressional Ethics. What are the most prominent differences between these two perspectives? Provide details from the text to support your answer.

3. Based on the viewpoints offered by G. Derek Musgrove and Armstrong Williams, do you believe that black members of Congress are singled out for ethics violations more often than their white counterparts? Why or why not?

Chapter 2

1. After reading the viewpoints expressed by Donald A. Brown and Mark A. Rothstein, do you believe that Congress should take an active role in helping to define the ethical dimensions of controversial social issues such as global warming or DNA testing?

2. Both Rushworth M. Kidder and David E. Skaggs argue that members of Congress can do a better job of exhibiting ethical behavior toward one another on Capitol Hill. What fundamental steps can be taken, according to Kidder and Skaggs, to promote a healthier atmosphere of civility and collegiality in Congress?

Chapter 3

1. Senator John McCain introduced legislation designed to restrict the access of lobbyists to members of the Senate, elements of which were eventually enacted as part of ongoing ethics reform measures in that legislative body. What are some of the unintended consequences that Randy Furst observes have arisen from limiting contact between lobbyists and members of Congress?

2. Knowing that Jack Abramoff is a former highly connected lobbyist who was convicted of mail fraud, conspiracy, and income tax evasion, how credible do you think his viewpoint is on the relationship between members of Congress and lobbying firms? Explain your reasoning.

3. Why does the Democratic Policy Committee hail the Honest Leadership and Open Government Act of 2007 as an important milestone in the effort to reform the influence of lobbyists on members of Congress? What are some of Bara Vaida's reservations about the actual enforcement of the new law?

Chapter 4

1. According to Chris Good, in what way does the news media succeed while congressional ethics committees typically fail when it comes to investigating and disciplining members of Congress who have been caught in a sex scandal?

2. Julian E. Zelizer documents a number of Congress members who have been involved in sex scandals and yet have been reelected and continued to serve effectively in office. Do you think it is easier or harder for a member of Congress to survive a sex scandal in the Internet age? Why? What does Gail Russell Chaddock suggest are some new ethical considerations for Congress members who use the Internet and social media to facilitate a sexual affair?

3. An effective system of financial disclosure is a key factor in determining whether members of Congress are engaging in insider trading or any other form of financial wrongdoing. In what ways do Jim Galloway and Daniel Gross describe the effectiveness—or lack thereof—of Congress's present system of financial disclosure? In 2012, Congress passed the Stop Trading on Congressional Knowledge Act (STOCK Act), which makes the financial disclosure process more transparent to the public. Do you think this law will help prevent future financial corruption in Congress? Why or why not?

Organizations to Contact

The editors have compiled the following list of organizations concerned with the issues debated in this book. The descriptions are derived from materials provided by the organizations. All have publications or information available for interested readers. The list was compiled on the date of publication of the present volume; the information provided here may change. Be aware that many organizations take several weeks or longer to respond to inquiries, so allow as much time as possible.

Campaign Legal Center (CLC)
215 E Street NE, Washington, DC 20002
(202) 736-2200 • fax: (202) 736-2222
e-mail: info@campaignlegalcenter.org
website: www.campaignlegalcenter.org

The Campaign Legal Center (CLC) is a nonprofit research and public advocacy group that examines the legal issues surrounding campaign finance, governmental transparency, and the ethical conduct of public officeholders. CLC provides policy and ethics programs designed to promote compliance with the regulations governing ethical conduct in the federal government. The group also leads the Congressional Ethics Coalition, a network of government watchdog organizations devoted to the reform of ethical standards in Congress. On its website, CLC publishes blogs, fact sheets, weekly reports, and articles of interest on current cases, as well as analyses of the Federal Election Commission's proceedings, campaign finance reform, and redistricting initiatives.

Center for Responsive Politics (CRP)
1101 Fourteenth Street NW, Suite 1030
Washington, DC 20005-5635
(202) 857-0044 • fax: (202) 857-7809
e-mail: info@crp.org
website: www.opensecrets.org

The Center for Responsive Politics tracks money in politics and its effect on public policy. Its website, OpenSecrets.org, provides detailed information on funding sources for presidential and congressional incumbents and challengers, as well as political action committees (PACs) and 527 committees. The center publishes the newsletter *Capital Eye* and numerous reports, including "The Millionaire on the Ballot" and "Shopping in (Partisan) Style," which are available on its website.

Citizens Against Government Waste (CAGW)
1301 Pennsylvania Avenue NW, Suite 1075
Washington, DC   20004
(202) 467-5300 • fax: (202) 467-4253
e-mail: membership@cagw.org
website: www.cagw.org

Citizens Against Government Waste (CAGW) is a private, nonpartisan, nonprofit organization that seeks to eliminate all forms of inefficiency, mismanagement, and waste of taxpayer dollars in the federal government. Considered a key source of information on government waste, the group maintains a membership of more than a million supporters nationwide. In addition to producing reports and articles on wasteful spending, inefficiency, and corruption, CAGW publishes *Government WasteWatch*, a quarterly newsletter for its members, and the *Congressional Pig Book Summary*, a highly regarded annual report on the most wasteful and irresponsible earmark spending projects proposed by members of Congress.

Citizens for Responsibility and Ethics
in Washington (CREW)
1400 Eye Street NW, Suite 450, Washington, DC   20005
(202) 408-5565
website: www.citizensforethics.org

Citizens for Responsibility and Ethics in Washington (CREW) is a nonprofit government watchdog organization that seeks to promote ethics and accountability in public service by exposing the unscrupulous conduct of government officials who serve special interest groups instead of the American public. The group uses research, litigation, and media outreach to bring the unethical conduct of members of Congress to the attention of the public. On its website, CREW publishes a number of essays and reports on dishonesty and corruption in government, including "Funds and Favors: Exposing Donors' Influence on Committee Leaders" and "No Strings Attached: How Former Members Spend Their Excess Campaign Funds." The website also features blogs, newsletters, press releases, and legal filings that document CREW's mission to expose government corruption.

Common Cause
1133 Nineteenth Street NW, 9th Floor
Washington, DC 20036
(202) 833-1200
e-mail: grassroots@commoncause.org
website: www.commoncause.org

Founded in 1970, Common Cause is a nonprofit, nonpartisan advocacy group. Its goal is to hold elected leaders accountable to the American people. Common Cause promotes a variety of activist causes such as campaign finance reform, voter registration drives, and openness in government. It has led voter mobilization drives prior to presidential elections and efforts to enact public financing of elections at the state level. Its website has an archive of its online journal, *Common Cause Magazine,* and links to other publications, including research papers, press releases, and blogs.

Democracy 21
2000 Massachusetts Avenue NW, Washington, DC 20036
(202) 355-9600 • fax: (202) 355-9606
e-mail: info@democracy21.org
website: www.democracy21.org

Founded in 1997 by former Common Cause president Fred Wertheimer, Democracy 21 works to eliminate the undue influence of big money in American politics and to ensure the integrity and fairness of government decisions and elections. The organization promotes campaign finance reform and other political reforms to accomplish these goals. On its website, Democracy 21 publishes issue papers on the Bipartisan Campaign Reform Act, public financing, the Federal Election Commission, and 527 organizations.

Institute for Global Ethics (IGE)
18 Central Street, Suite 2B, Rockport, ME   04856
(207) 236-6658 • fax: (207) 236-6614
e-mail: ethics@globalethics.org
website: www.globalethics.org

Founded in 1990, the Institute for Global Ethics (IGE) is an independent, nonprofit organization that promotes ethical behavior and moral action in institutions and nations around the world. The group employs research, public advocacy, and the practical application of its values to encourage a culture of integrity at individual, governmental, and national levels. IGE's principal publication is *Ethics Newsline*, an online weekly digest of worldwide news related to ethics in business, government, and society.

Judicial Watch
425 Third Street SW, Suite 800, Washington, DC   20024
(888) 593-8442 • fax: (202) 646-5199
e-mail: info@judicialwatch.org
website: www.judicialwatch.org

Judicial Watch is a conservative, nonpartisan educational foundation that advocates the need for greater accountability, ethical conduct, and transparency among government and judicial officials. The group employs litigation, investigations, and public awareness campaigns to hold officials accountable for unethical conduct in public service. Judicial Watch publishes the findings of its investigations in a monthly publication, *The Verdict*, as well as in special reports, legal filings, and other educational materials that the group makes available on its website.

National Legal and Policy Center (NLPC)
107 Park Washington Court, Falls Church, VA   22046
(703) 237-1970 • fax: (703) 237-2090
website: nlpc.org

Founded in 1991, the National Legal and Policy Center
(NLPC) is committed to improving the ethical conduct of
public officials through research, investigation, litigation, and
public awareness campaigns. The group believes that the best
way to foster a culture of ethical responsibility among elected
officials is to reduce the size of government to limit opportu-
nities for corruption. The NLPC publishes a series of special
reports on its website that addresses a wide range of topics associated with corporate, government, and union corruption.

Office of Congressional Ethics (OCE)
US House of Representatives, Washington, DC   20024
(202) 225-9739 • fax: (202) 226-0997
e-mail: oce@mail.house.gov
website: oce.house.gov

Formed in 2008 by the US House of Representatives as an independent investigative agency, the Office of Congressional
Ethics (OCE) is composed of a nonpartisan panel of private
citizens who review allegations of ethical impropriety against
members of the House and their staffs. The OCE does not
have jurisdiction over the US Senate, the executive branch
(including the president), or the judicial branch. The OCE is
not authorized to counsel House members on proper ethical
conduct, to determine the veracity of an ethics violation, or to
recommend sanctions against an alleged ethics violator. The
panel can only review allegations of ethical misconduct and
present the findings of its investigation to the US House Committee on Ethics for further action. The OCE website provides
a variety of information for interested parties, including a
citizens' guide, quarterly reports, referrals, and press adviso-
ries.

Sunlight Foundation
1818 N Street NW, Suite 300, Washington, DC   20036
(202) 742-1520
website: www.sunlightfoundation.com

The Sunlight Foundation is a nonprofit, nonpartisan organization that seeks to gain greater government transparency through the use of twenty-first-century technology. With a board and advisory group made up of the heads of major American corporations, the Sunlight Foundation offers grants to organizations that use the Internet to provide Americans with greater access to the workings of their government. The Sunlight Foundation supports a number of initiatives that concern congressional ethics and governmental transparency, including transparency in earmark spending, honest financial industry reporting, and the increased disclosure of lobbying activity on Capitol Hill.

US House Committee on Ethics
1015 Longworth House Office Building (LHOB)
Washington, DC   20515
(202) 225-7103 • fax: (202) 225-7392
website: ethics.house.gov

Created in 1967, the US House Committee on Ethics, also known as the House Ethics Committee, is responsible for upholding the rules and regulations found in the Code of Official Conduct for the House of Representatives. Consisting of ten panelists, it is the only House committee that is required to divide itself evenly between members of the Democratic and Republican Parties. The committee enforces the ethical conduct of House members and their staffs, investigates alleged ethical and/or legal infractions committed by House members and their staffs, and proposes disciplinary action for alleged violators to the full House for its consideration. The committee typically focuses on such abuses of office as the improper acceptance of travel, the unsanctioned receipt of gifts, dishonesty in making financial disclosures, and the accumulation of questionable outside income. The committee's website features a wealth of information for interested members of the public, including press releases, information on financial disclosures, and reports on committee proceedings.

US Senate Select Committee on Ethics

220 Hart Building, Washington, DC   20510
(202) 224-2981 • fax: (202) 224-7416
website: www.ethics.senate.gov

Established in 1964, the US Senate Select Committee on Ethics, also known as the Senate Ethics Committee, is authorized by the full Senate to accept and investigate allegations of ethical misconduct committed by the legislative body's members, officers, and staff. Further, the committee has the responsibility of recommending disciplinary action to the full Senate or reporting violations of the law to the proper authorities for those members who are proven to have violated any part of the Senate Code of Official Conduct. The committee also has the authority to propose amendments to the Code of Official Conduct to ensure that the Senate adheres to a high standard of ethics. The committee investigates a wide range of ethics violations, including unauthorized disclosures of intelligence information, abuse of franking (i.e., mailing) privileges, failure to disclose pertinent financial information, and unauthorized gifts to or from foreign dignitaries. The website for the US Senate Select Committee on Ethics supplies interested parties with key information on the group's overall function, including an overview of the financial disclosure process, annual reports, press releases, and training documentation.

Bibliography of Books

Jack Abramoff   *Capitol Punishment: The Hard Truth About Washington Corruption from America's Most Notorious Lobbyist.* Washington, DC: WND Books, 2011.

Citizens Against Government Waste   *2012 Congressional Pig Book Summary.* Washington, DC: Citizens Against Government Waste, 2012.

Jason P. Collins, ed.   *Congressional Conduct, Ethics, and the Rangel Investigation.* Hauppauge, NY: Nova Science Publishers, 2011.

Robert Draper   *Do Not Ask What Good We Do: Inside the U.S. House of Representatives.* New York: Free Press, 2012.

Scott A. Frisch and Sean Q. Kelly   *Cheese Factories on the Moon: Why Earmarks Are Good for American Democracy.* Boulder, CO: Paradigm Publishers, 2011.

Deanna Gelak   *Lobbying and Advocacy: Winning Strategies, Resources, Recommendations, Ethics and Ongoing Compliance for Lobbyists and Washington Advocates: The Best of Everything Lobbying and Washington Advocacy.* Alexandria, VA: TheCapitol.Net Inc., 2008.

Joseph Gibson   *A Better Congress: Change the Rules, Change the Results.* Alexandria, VA: Two Seas Media, 2010.

David V.
Gotlfried, ed.
Earmarks: Budgetary Pork or Butter?
Hauppauge, NY: Nova Science
Publishers, 2008.

Robert G. Kaiser
*So Damn Much Money: The Triumph
of Lobbying and the Corrosion of
American Government.* New York:
Vintage Books, 2010.

Sheila Kennedy
and David
Schultz
*American Public Service:
Constitutional and Ethical
Foundations.* Sudbury, MA: Jones &
Bartlett Publishers, 2011.

Rushworth M.
Kidder
*The Ethics Recession: Reflections on
the Moral Underpinnings of the
Current Economic Crisis.* Rockport,
ME: Institute for Global Ethics, 2009.

Frances E. Lee
*Beyond Ideology: Politics, Principles,
and Partisanship in the U.S. Senate.*
Chicago, IL: University of Chicago
Press, 2009.

Lawrence Lessig
*Republic, Lost: How Money Corrupts
Congress—and a Plan to Stop It.* New
York: Twelve, 2011.

Bertram J. Levine
*The Art of Lobbying: Building Trust
and Selling Policy.* Washington, DC:
CQ Press, 2009.

Gary Lee Malecha
and Daniel J.
Reagan
*The Public Congress: Congressional
Deliberation in a New Media Age.*
New York: Routledge, 2012.

Thomas E. Mann and Norman J. Ornstein — *The Broken Branch: How Congress Is Failing America and How to Get It Back on Track*. New York: Oxford University Press, 2006.

Alan L. Moss — *Selling Out America's Democracy: How Lobbyists, Special Interests, and Campaign Financing Undermine the Will of the People*. Westport, CT: Praeger Publishers, 2008.

George Derek Musgrove — *Rumor, Repression, and Racial Politics: How the Harassment of Black Elected Officials Shaped Post-Civil Rights America*. Athens: University of Georgia Press, 2012.

Walter J. Oleszek — *Congressional Procedures and the Policy Process*. 8th ed. Washington, DC: CQ Press, 2010.

Richard W. Painter — *Getting the Government America Deserves: How Ethics Reform Can Make a Difference*. New York: Oxford University Press, 2009.

Peter Schweizer — *Throw Them All Out: How Politicians and Their Friends Get Rich off Insider Stock Tips, Land Deals, and Cronyism That Would Send the Rest of Us to Prison*. Boston, MA: Houghton Mifflin Harcourt, 2011.

Marcus Stern, Jerry Kammer, Dean Calbreath, and George E. Condon Jr. — *The Wrong Stuff: The Extraordinary Saga of Randy "Duke" Cunningham, the Most Corrupt Congressman Ever Caught*. New York: PublicAffairs, 2007.

Peter H. Stone	*Casino Jack and the United States of Money: Superlobbyist Jack Abramoff and the Buying of Washington.* New York: Farrar, Straus and Giroux, 2006.
Dennis F. Thompson	*Ethics in Congress: From Individual to Institutional Corruption.* Washington, DC: Brookings Institution, 1995.
Susan J. Tolchin and Martin Tolchin	*Glass Houses: Congressional Ethics and the Politics of Venom.* Boulder, CO: Westview Press, 2004.

Index

A

"Abnormal Returns from the Common Stock Investments of Members of the US House of Representatives" (report), 202–203, 207

Abramoff, Jack
    as cautionary tale/example, 171
    lobbying and ethics reform does not address cause of unethical activity, 140–143
    scandals, 44, 60, 140, 145, 155
    See also Lobbying

Absolute power, 82

Accountability
    ethics and lobbying reform legislation proposals, 135, 146
    open government, 165–166
    tenure, and ethics considerations, 73, 76, 80
    waning/endangered, in Congress, 75, 107–108, 110–111
    See also Transparency

ACORN, 75

Advisory letters and functions, Senate Ethics Committee, 33–34, 41

African American lawmakers. *See* Race issues

AIG, 69, 71, 109

Alaska, 131–132

Allentown Morning Call (newspaper), 114

Americans with Disabilities Act (1990), 99, 103

Anti-environmental thought and policy, 88–94

Appropriations bills, and ethics reform, 131, 132–133, 134, 136, 139
    See also Earmarks

Archer Daniels Midland, 158

Arcuri, Michael, 75

Assassination attempts, 119

Austin, Texas, 214

B

Bachus, Spencer, 200, 202

Bailouts. *See* Financial bailouts

Baird, Brian, 176, 206, 209

Baker, Robert G. "Bobby," 23, 24, 26–27, 28

Barnes, Fred, 124–128

Bass, Gary, 155

Bauman, Robert, 190

Baumann, Nick, 112–117

Bear Stearns, 109

Berke, Elliot S., 48

Berkley, Shelley, 15, 16–17

Bernanke, Ben, 200, 202

Biotechnology legislation, 95–105

Bipartisanship
    ethics committee rosters, 24–25, 76
    Genetic Information Nondiscrimination Act support, 96
    human dimension, 121

P

R